An Innocent Child

Also by Toni Maguire

Silent Child
Please Protect Us
No Going Home
Won't You Love Me?
Why, Father?
Abandoned Child
Don't Tell Mummy
When Daddy Comes Home
Nobody Came
Don't You Love Your Daddy?
Can't Anyone Help Me?
They Stole My Innocence
Pretty Maids All In A Row
Daddy's Little Girl

An Innocent Child

TONI MAGUIRE

with GEORGIA TURNER

jb

First published in the UK by John Blake Publishing
An imprint of The Zaffre Publishing Group
A Bonnier Books UK company
4th Floor, Victoria House
Bloomsbury Square,
London, WC1B 4DA
England

Owned by Bonnier Books
Sveavägen 56, Stockholm, Sweden

www.facebook.com/johnblakebooks
twitter.com/jblakebooks

Paperback – 978-1-789467-62-8
eBook – 978-1-789467-61-1

A CIP catalogue of this book is available from the British Library.

Design by www.envydesign.co.uk
Printed and bound in Great Britain by Clays Ltd, Elcograf S.p.A.

1 3 5 7 9 10 8 6 4 2

*For each paperback book sold, Bonnier Books UK shall donate 2.5% of its net
receipts to the NSPCC (registered charity numbers 216401 and SC037717).*

The authors of this work want to show Georgia Turner's experience growing up and
so you will find language in this book which may be offensive. It is used to show the
reality of the author's experience and they and the Publisher would like to add a
trigger warning for that here.

This book is a work of non-fiction, based on the life, experiences and recollections
of Georgia Turner. Certain details in this story, including names and locations, have been
changed to protect the identity and privacy of the authors, their family and
those mentioned.

John Blake Publishing is an imprint of Bonnier Books UK
www.bonnierbooks.co.uk

To my boys. The first words that come to mind: I am truly, deeply sorry. I wanted my story out there for you to hear my version of events and for other women suffering at the hands of violent men. If I was only a time traveller, you would be here with me today. I have never stopped loving nor thinking about all three of you. I pray that you find it in your hearts to forgive me.

Mum x

To my family. I am sorry for the pain and heartache I have caused you to endure. Nan, I am sorry for not taking your advice and positive criticism. I would like to thank you for your support throughout my life and I am forever grateful.

To Toni.

Thank you for writing my story and helping me get it out publicly. It hasn't been easy going over my past traumas and it has triggered a lot of emotions inside but you have guided and supported me every step of the way. I am forever grateful to you.

This book is a work of non-fiction based on the life, experiences and recollections of the author. The names of people, places, dates, sequences or the details of events have been changed to protect the privacy and identity of the author and her children.

Contents

Preface	*ix*
Chapter 1	*1*
Chapter 2	*5*
Chapter 3	*11*
Chapter 4	*17*
Chapter 5	*24*
Chapter 6	*31*
Chapter 7	*41*
Chapter 8	*46*
Chapter 9	*52*
Chapter 10	*56*
Chapter 11	*61*
Chapter 12	*68*
Chapter 13	*74*
Chapter 14	*81*
Chapter 15	*96*
Chapter 16	*102*
Chapter 17	*107*
Chapter 18	*111*
Chapter 19	*116*
Chapter 20	*124*
Chapter 21	*126*
Chapter 22	*128*

Chapter 23	133
Chapter 24	137
Chapter 25	142
Chapter 26	145
Chapter 27	150
Chapter 28	152
Chapter 29	155
Chapter 30	169
Chapter 31	176
Chapter 32	179
Chapter 33	186
Chapter 34	190
Chapter 35	194
Chapter 36	201
Chapter 37	208
Chapter 38	211
Chapter 39	214
Chapter 40	221
Chapter 41	229
Chapter 42	232
Chapter 43	244
Chapter 44	251
Chapter 45	256
Chapter 46	258
Chapter 47	274
Chapter 48	280
Chapter 49	287
Chapter 50	289
Chapter 51	295
Chapter 52	303
Acknowledgements	307

Preface

It was about a year ago when Georgia, having read my books, decided to write to me. Her story was, I thought, quite amazing. The moment I read her emails, I was of the opinion that not only did she have a troubled childhood, but an early adult one as well. When I read all her notes I could tell that to turn her life around when she reached her mid-twenties took tremendous courage.

One part of her story that particularly caught my attention was that her maternal grandfather had been an associate of the notorious East London gangster brothers, the Krays. Not that he had mixed with them once he moved from the area. What would have made him stand out, though, was that he was the best man at 'Mad' Frankie Fraser's wedding. I suspect you might not have heard of him, but he was one of the Kray brothers' henchmen, one who would spend a great deal of time in prison for the work he carried out on their behalf.

As I read more about him, I could understand why Frankie

was called 'Mad' Frankie. Back then, there had been photos of his marriage, which appeared in all the newspapers and, of course, the good-looking best man would have been in them too. It seems the press simply loved writing about families with a life of crime and many of the newspaper features that appeared later in the timeline of Georgia's grandfather's life would certainly have caused questions to be raised. It was those questions that I believe introduced some of the family's problems that I read about in the letters Georgia sent to me.

From what I know, Georgia's grandfather only knew the twins because he grew up near them. No, he did not work for them, nor did he have anything to do with their crimes, but that didn't stop some people from talking about him. Those remarks seem to have had a ripple effect on his daughter, who became Georgia's mother.

So here, finally, is Georgia's story …

1

When did my story begin? The answer is around 40 years before I came into this world. I can remember the day when I was little more than seven, when our family's lives changed and darkness enveloped us. Ever since, I have wanted to know more about why that happened.

Over the last few years, I have spent time searching for more information on our family. I've written notes as I found some of the information, but many of the answers had already been stored away deep in my subconscious for a very long time. I've gone through old photos and googled sections from newspapers, which helped me gain further understanding. But when I sit and daydream, I let random pictures of my early years float into my head and I have to say my memory tells me that it was just perfect back then.

I was the youngest of three children. My sister Lucy was three years older and my brother Sid is the eldest, being almost five years older than me. We were such a cheerful little trio, for we all felt that we were part of a loving family.

We had a mum who read us stories before she tucked us all up into our beds and a dad who had us taking turns to ride on his shoulders when we all went out for the day. We also had caring grandparents on my mum's side who lived nearby and enjoyed coming over and spoiling us rotten.

Then there were the birthdays and, with five of us living in the house, they seemed to come round pretty often. When it was one of our parents celebrating a birthday, our grandparents would arrive for the evening so they could look after us, while Mum and Dad went out for dinner alone so they could have some time on their own as a couple.

I can picture Mum now, with her thick blonde hair falling to her shoulders, as she came into the living room and said, 'Give us a twirl.' The last time I saw my parents going out together she was wearing a floaty blue dress and I thought she was just the most beautiful mummy we could ever have. When she bent down to kiss each of us goodnight, I could smell her favourite perfume and see the sparkle in her eyes before she straightened up and left the room with our proud dad, who smelt of soap, shampoo and his best aftershave.

When a birthday came round for one of us three, Mum would make a huge cake with candles on it that had to be blown out so that we could make a wish before 'Happy Birthday' was sung. Beside the cake would be a pile of presents that we could hardly wait to open.

But if birthdays were great, Christmas was even better. Being the youngest child, I believed in Father Christmas much longer than my brother and sister did, although I suspect they kept quiet about knowing so that our parents still continued to fill their stockings with presents. Being tucked into bed and kissed goodnight didn't stop me trying to stay awake because I had been told more than once by Lucy and Sid that Father Christmas would be coming down the chimney later to fill my stocking with gifts. We had left out mince pies for him, a bottle of whisky and a glass alongside for him to take a nip. Not that I knew that it was Dad who enjoyed them. Of course, at that age I had been expecting a jolly old man with a thick white beard, like the one I had met in one of the large London department stores, which made me want to stay awake to see him again. It was tough to try to stop my drooping eyes from closing, but I was determined to see him again. Inevitably I failed and, on waking, I can still remember the excitement I felt as my eyes opened and I saw the bulging stocking at the end of my bed.

It didn't take long for all three of us to wake and gather in the living room, dragging our stockings behind us. Soon, we were pulling our presents out. Small packets of sweets and our favourite chocolate bars were ripped open and we nibbled away. Being allowed sweet treats before breakfast for one day was all part of the joy of Christmas in our house.

When the three of us are together now, we think about how wonderful those early Christmases were, but it also makes us sad when we look back to those happy times when our house was filled with laughter as well as presents. We all loved the way it looked after Dad had put up the Christmas tree, with its twinkling lights, and the whole family helped to decorate it. After the tree was finished, Dad filled the room with fake snow.

Then there was the eagerly anticipated Christmas dinner

when our grandparents would arrive with still more parcels and food and drink contributions to add to the already groaning table and sideboard. Boxing Day was also great fun as Mum's younger sister, Clare, and her family would arrive. Aunt Clare was my favourite.

These days, there are still times when I lay curled up in bed and I can't help but picture our home as it was then, not only over Christmas but other times as well. With its pretty decor and happy atmosphere, it was just lovely. Outside the front room window there was a large magnolia tree, which looked so beautiful when its tight buds opened and huge pink and white flowers covered it in the early days of spring. The garden had flowers and shrubs that Mum enjoyed tending to and I remember Dad putting up a swing for us to play on. He and Mum would push us on it until we learnt how to get it moving by ourselves.

Yes, those were happy days. Sadly, that life together all ended abruptly. It seemed to happen at the same time as I began going to school. Young as I was, I could feel that all that happiness in our home had slunk out of the windows and under the doors. All three of us kids felt that a cloud of darkness had fallen over our bright lives. And young as we were, we realised that everything was changing.

2

When I entered my teens, my brother and sister and I wanted to understand the reasons why our lives had gone so wrong at such a young age. We discussed some of the contributing factors, but it has taken me a long time to work out some of the more subtle answers as to what had caused the breakdown of our family. It is that which makes me understand why I say that my story began long before I came into this world.

To begin that tale, I'm going to take you back to the time when my grandfather was a young man. He had been such an important part of my life, right up to a few years ago when he passed. Through all the years I knew him, he was my hero. Not only was he a tall, handsome man, but he was also a strong one, both physically and emotionally. He would never have let someone make him do anything he did not approve of. A brilliant businessman, he had an excellent reputation for being honest and doing an excellent job at a fair price. He was also a wonderful family man, who over the years did his best for each one of us.

It was my Aunt Clare who told me a little about his early years, which made me see what a remarkable man my grandfather had grown into. What I don't know is whether his father died in the Second World War, or if he had just left his wife. I asked her one day, but my aunt didn't seem to know either.

'What was Grandad's mother like, Aunt Clare?'

'She was certainly poor, I do know that. For some reason, when so many children were evacuated into the countryside during the war years, he stayed with her despite the East End suffering catastrophic bombing at the hands of the German Luftwaffe. I'm sure that there must have been days when they were shivering with cold and hunger as they listened to the planes flying over. You know how you suddenly see a block of flats in the middle of a row of terraced houses? Well, that's because a bomb had hit the houses that once stood there. When my dad started school, he would hardly have looked smart, but then a lot of children didn't – it took a long while after the war for the poor to start living better lives. Goodness knows how Dad's mum managed. All that bombing must have been so frightening, as well as having to spend nights in the bomb shelters praying that their home would still be there in the morning. Those years were a terrible time for so many and so many Londoners died.'

I shuddered at the thought of how bad Grandad's life must have been as a little boy.

'His mother must have been brave,' was all I said then.

'What I do know about my father,' continued Clare, 'was that when he was still young, he had the will to succeed.

He was determined to ignore the fact that spending his early years in a squalid little flat meant that life had dealt him a bad hand. When I started school, he said the same things to me as he told your mum. That I was to concentrate on my education, as he had, because it was the golden key to my future. He strongly believed in the saying that "education gives you knowledge and knowledge sets you free". What made him different from others of his generation and class was that he believed girls should work, as hard at school as boys – "If women want to work then they can, and if they want to help their children learn, then they need to know a lot more than just cooking and sewing," was another one of his sayings that your mum and I heard pretty often.'

'Well, he's a good businessman.'

'He is that. Do you know what he told me once? That when he was only 12, he had already worked out what he was going to do when he left school. He looked around at the devastation in the East End and saw endless opportunities. He wanted to earn good money so he could help his mother – that took quite a few years.'

'So, was it building he was thinking of even then, Clare?' I asked, fascinated by what she was telling me.

'It was. He could see that houses were being repaired in almost every street, while blocks of flats and prefabs were being put up on the bombsites. He could tell that a good deal of the country needed new homes and building them would go on for years. As he lived in the part of London where so many homes had been destroyed, I guess he saw his future right there.'

It was Nan who told me recently a little more about the man she had sadly outlived. I can still see her upright figure all dressed in black at his funeral. She must have been heartbroken for he was the love of her life, but Nan had courage. She came from a generation who managed to hide their feelings well and appeared stoic as she mourned the loss of her husband of so many years. It took her a while before she was able to tell me about their time together – when they met and how the early years of their marriage had been. Her eyes took on a misty look as she explained how he had worked so hard to give her the best of everything he could provide. Her eyes drifted to the mantelpiece where there was a wedding photo and one taken at their golden wedding anniversary; a wintry smile tinged her lips.

'He was so determined that we would have a good life together,' she went on. Her face took on a glow and her eyes shone as she talked about the man she loved. 'And we did. I wasn't convinced that he was the right person for me when we first met, but it didn't take long for me to decide that he was. I could hardly believe it when he told me that the very moment he first saw me, he knew I was the one he was going to marry. He wanted us to have a nice home and so he worked as hard as he could to provide one.'

She brought out her wedding album then; it had yellowed with age, but the black-and-white formally posed photos were lovely. As I sat on the sofa next to her, she talked me through each one. I saw a tall, good-looking man and a petite, pretty woman who looked equally happy.

'We had to live with his mum for a while, but it didn't take your grandad long to save up enough for us to rent a flat. Back then, people were content to be renters, but not him. He wanted to buy it and, a year later, he did. He put in a new kitchen and bathroom then decorated it from top to toe. We didn't stay there long, though; his aim was to do it up well and then sell it on for a tidy profit so we could afford to move into our first house. He said that our children needed a garden to play in instead of a street. So, by the time your mum arrived, the flat had been sold and we moved. It was ten years later when your Aunt Clare arrived and by then, we already had this place, which was even better than the first house and in a nicer area for his "girls".'

I smiled then because 'this place', as Nan called it, was a large Victorian house in a smart street. It had enough bedrooms for the whole family to move into if they wanted to.

Nan told me a little more about how Grandad had done so well in the building trade. He might have started off by doing odd jobs, but he watched others and soon learnt a lot about the trade – 'He set up his own small company and I watched it grow.'

By the time I came along, Grandad's company had become a large one. There were certainly a lot of people working for him – plasterers, decorators, electricians, plumbers – in fact, just about every trade to improve old houses and build new ones. The East End was being gentrified even then and my grandfather was ahead of the game: buying wrecks, doing them up to a high standard and then selling them on for a high profit.

I'm guessing that, once he had his business bringing in

good money, Grandad hadn't changed much over the years. He still looked after his daughters and us, his grandchildren. I had seen the photos of him when he was a very attractive young man, but it was the elderly one I had loved so much.

The one thing that Nan didn't want to talk about was the people that Grandad had known well from his past. Let's just say the wrong people, though I doubt if he knew that to begin with. Nor would he have ever thought of the harm that knowing them might do to his family.

3

When Grandad was young, he came to know a pair of glamorous and apparently charming twins, the Krays. I'm sure that many of you reading this book will have seen at least one of the films or documentaries on their lives or read about them, or will at least have heard just how chilling their crimes were.

Like most people of my age group, I've seen films where handsome actors play the part of the Krays, while glamorous actresses play their vulnerable, doe-eyed girlfriends. Those films showed the two sides of the twins: one side was all charm and charisma while the other was cold and brutal. Now I can only wish that I had remembered at least one of those films when 20 years ago, at the age of 17, I was seduced by a man called Desmond, who also possessed charm and charisma in abundance. At the time I had not understood his reasons for wanting me to be with him. If only I had, my life might have been very different. I should have remembered those films and they might have explained some of his magnetic traits. It hadn't taken long for me to see Desmond's charm disappear, only to be replaced by threats. And all those films had caused people to remember the past, which meant gossip was flashing around. Anyone who mixed with the Krays and their inner circle could hardly have been innocent was the growing sentiment when Mum first went to school.

It was my Aunt Clare who explained a few things about Mum to me.

'She was a nervous child at school. Remember, Georgia, that I only arrived there when she was near to leaving, but we sensed it at home. She was such a pretty girl that teachers couldn't help smiling at her. But you know how groups of school children, especially teenagers, can be. They don't see any harm in teasing and, boy, did they tease her. She didn't realise that it was all meant in fun and so she got really upset. Later, I was told that your mum had been teased since she was small, but as she grew older, it became more targeted and hurtful. That meant her concentration in class and on her homework became more and more difficult. She was bright, though – I heard from one of the teachers how good she had been at writing essays. She could have been a writer, she told me. It was when she was in her teens that the teasing became more vicious, more like bullying.'

Someone had spread a rumour that Mum's father knew the Krays. Not that she herself knew anything about the twins – our parents never spoke about them. The boys at school started saying that they didn't want to be seen talking to anyone whose dad had known monsters and murderers. Mum got so angry at the thought of her father being insulted and once clenched her fist and thumped the ringleader hard. Of course, that didn't please the teachers and she was punished. I don't think she understood that those boys were just joking with her – you know, doing their best to wind her up.'

'Did she have a boyfriend before she met Dad?' I asked.

'I think she had a couple of dates with boys, but it never lasted long,' said Clare. 'From what I heard, she was well into her teens when boys at school started asking her out and she didn't think they meant it. She thought it was just so they could get at her.

'There were always lots of rumours going around. One was that there was a block of flats locally that had the bodies of the Krays' victims buried in the foundations. Your mum was asked if her dad was the builder who had hidden them in the concrete. It was stupid to get upset about that as Dad was never involved in building high-rise tower blocks. The councils employed specialist builders for that and I'm sure they would have known if there was a body there. She should have laughed it off – that's what I did when I heard that same story repeated several times over the years.'

'But why didn't she, Aunt Clare?'

'She was intelligent – you should see some of the essays and poems she wrote. But not sharp, she wasn't capable of putting anyone in their place. She thought when people came up with some gossip, they meant it, but mostly, they didn't. All it needed was a sharp response, but your mother wasn't able to do that. I did try and talk to her about it when I was old enough to be friends with her, but she hardly listened.

'I can understand her wanting to find the right man.

She should have noticed how many men kept glancing over at her. Do you know how pretty she was? But she never took them seriously.'

'Yes, I have some photos of her when she was young. She looked beautiful, and innocent too.'

'And then she met your dad. Now I'm not saying anything against him, but he wasn't the right man for her, was he?'

I could hardly disagree. I can describe my young mother from looking at the photos I have of her. She had thick blonde hair, large sapphire-blue eyes and such a captivating smile; I thought she was just so beautiful then.

It's hard to believe what would happen to her looks only years later.

The mother I knew was far from confident. Even with the support my grandparents gave her, she never seemed able to sort her life out. Seeing her beautiful young face in the photos nearly brings me to tears. I go through the photo albums which she had kept and I saw us three when we were small children. Some of our relatives also feature but I noticed there were few of my mum's friends in any of them. No wedding photographs of my parents. But then I think about how she was married.

Her parents, my grandparents, loved her a lot. I knew from the stories they told me about her that they always doted on her and just wanted the best for her. It was only when, glowing with happiness, she told them she had met the right person and introduced Dad to them that they were not very happy. Straight away, Grandad sensed that this man was not going to be right for his 20-year-old daughter.

I've seen photos of Dad then and, yes, he was good

looking. No wonder my mother was swept off her feet. But my grandfather was a shrewd man – he must have hoped that my dad would disappear off the scene. He told Nan that first night that he knew he was the wrong person and, in the end, he would give their daughter grief.

Dad must have been told by Mum that her father wasn't pleased with her choice. My grandparents were just as horrified when, without saying a word, my parents were married in the registry office – people off the street were brought in as witnesses. Later that day, they came back and told my grandparents they were now a married couple. I should think my grandparents must have gritted their teeth and tried their best to congratulate them.

What on earth was Mum thinking to marry without telling anyone? So typical of her, though. I suppose she knew that news of the marriage would not be welcome. Seeing as she still lived at home, it's a wonder that her parents weren't angrier. They must have felt that Mum and Dad had defiantly gone behind their backs as they had already rented a small flat to live in. I'm sure my parents, in turn, expected Grandad to relent and to put his hand in his pocket and buy them a decent place to live in. But as I said, he was a shrewd man. If his new son-in-law wanted him to help, he was going to have to prove himself and work for it. Grandad offered him a well-paid job in his company, which Dad accepted and apparently, give him his dues, he worked hard. Grandad waited a while before he sat them both down and told them he had seen a house that he thought they would like living in – 'Our builders will make sure everything is right there.'

While the pair looked pleased, Grandad also made it clear that this was not a gift. He told them that he would put down a sizeable deposit and, with the wages Dad was now earning, there would be no problem with the bank granting a mortgage. As I said, my grandfather was a shrewd man and, although he could have paid for the house outright, he had wanted his new son-in-law to be responsible for the monthly payments. I'm sure that this arrangement must have come as a disappointment to the newlyweds, but then Grandad was a man who had worked hard for everything he owned and he expected any man in his family to do the same.

Dad turned out to be quite a good decorator and quickly learnt about the other building trades done by the company. The house they moved into was the one I told you about earlier – the one that we loved living in, and the one we were made to leave when I was seven.

4

We all knew that Grandad's company had been asked to modernise a very large house just up the road from us. It was a big job and both Mum and Dad seemed quite excited that he had handed the job over to Dad to manage himself with a team of men under him.

'I'll be earning good money on that one,' I heard Dad say more than once. 'They want an extension built at the back and the attic made into another bedroom, then there's a new kitchen and bathrooms. When that's finished, it will need redecorating. Be there for months with a team.'

Dad must have forgotten that his wife knew a lot about building works, having grown up around her father's workers.

'Good money's about right! Her husband's loaded and she wants to show off to all the neighbours,' Mum said, smiling. 'But it won't take long to get all that work done, not with the team Dad's given you.'

'I think it might – she seems to know exactly what she wants done and each time she adds extra bits onto the job, the bill grows. No skimping there!'

'Oh, I know Lorraine – she's not that fussy, it just has to look good.'

'So, you know her, do you?' Dad asked.

'Yes, we got friendly a while back when they first moved in. She's fun.'

As he also had found her 'fun', Dad said nothing more. Not that Mum was aware that he was having an affair with Lorraine – none of us were, at least not then.

So, why can I remember so much detail about a thread of conversation that most children would ignore? It was because we three kids found it upsetting that, once he began work at Lorraine's, massive arguments started between our parents. Hearing them snap and shout at each other was unsettling for us all.

'Why are you so late?' I heard Mum ask crossly and him telling her angrily to stop her nagging. 'Your team would have left long ago,' she persisted, 'so, why did you stay longer?'

'You're wrong, Paula,' he countered. 'We're all putting in extra hours and working as hard as we can.'

'Oh yeah? You've probably been sat around, having a drink with her so you can make my father think you're working more hours than you are. You're trying to get more money out of this job, aren't you?'

Dad must have been a bit relieved that her suspicions concerned cash, not sex.

'No, don't be stupid! There's a fixed price – any extras she wants are quoted for.'

Mum snorted then, for she knew enough to know that

fixed prices could be changed a little.

It was Grandad who found out about the affair a while before Mum did. Dad might have kidded his wife that he was still working, but Grandad knew that there was little work left for him to do. No doubt Mum must have said something that made him suspicious for he drove over to have a look at the job and immediately guessed what was happening.

He had met Lorraine, who with her long, thick red hair, bright-green eyes and smashing figure, meant he understood why his son-in-law might be interested in her. He had also heard that she was a huge flirt and enjoyed flashing the kind of smile that drew men to her. His men told him that she was often half-dressed when they arrived in the morning, which again rang alarm bells.

When Grandad reached the house where Lorraine lived, he saw that Dad had blocked a neighbour's drive with the company work van. As it had his name and business telephone number on it, he recognised it straight away. There was no reason for Dad to have that van there. Grandad knew that the work on the house was just about complete and, if there were a few things to check, why take the company van? To fool his daughter, no doubt. Make her believe that he was working instead of her guessing that he was in bed with his client.

I know from what my mother told me much later that Grandad warned my dad to call off the affair or else he would tell Mum. Of course, my dad being a typical man, he chose to ignore him and didn't end it. As I later learnt, not many men do!

So, how did Mum find out? She, too, had become suspicious

and a few times she had walked to Lorraine's house just to see who was in there. She couldn't see any of the workmen, so she guessed it was just Dad there.

'Women,' she told me quite a few years later, 'can tell when their husbands are being unfaithful.'

It turned out it was she who told Grandad and not the other way around.

'I wanted to try and get him behaving,' was all she said to us then.

I noticed when we sat down to dinner that Mum was not eating much and kept jumping up from the table. At the time I was too young to understand why my mother had changed from a happy, curvy woman to a rather skinny, highly strung and unhappy one. I could feel that she was seething with anger although she was doing her best not to show it. Dad, on the other hand, looked fed up with her most of the time. To begin with he would come in from work, eat his meal and then I would hear him say, 'Got some more work to do, be back in a couple of hours.'

We all knew he would be out far longer than that.

That was when Lucy and I noticed Mum looking tearful.

'Gone to be with that woman,' my sister whispered to me. Being older than me, Lucy spotted a lot more than I did. 'That's why Mum's so unhappy,' she added knowingly.

I wasn't sure what she meant then, though it didn't take long for me to know all about the affair.

Not all my memories of that time are clear – after all, I was only seven. But I have one memory of being in the bedroom with Mum which has stayed in my mind for all these years.

She was standing in her bra and pants in front of the mirror, anxiously squeezing her admittedly small rolls of fat.

'I've got to get rid of these,' she sighed. 'Got to make myself eat less – no more bread or sweet stuff for me. You're going to help.'

For a moment I thought she must be talking to me or at least to her reflection in the mirror. But no, it was the pill in her hand she was addressing, the one that would take away her appetite. Into her mouth it went, one gulp and it was gone. I watched her smile once she was sure it went down. She patted her stomach then, saying, 'There you are. I'm going to be slim again, aren't I? That'll get him back.'

Turning, she saw me standing by the door with a puzzled look on my face and she laughed a little.

'You heard me talking to myself, didn't you?'

I nodded.

'Well, it's you three kids that have made me fat, isn't it?'

I didn't understand what she meant, but then laughing gaily for once, she knelt and put her arms around me.

'Means I'm going to be a better mum soon,' she said more than once as she squeezed me tightly and kissed the top of my head. 'You're such a lovely child,' she told me as another hug came my way.

I know now she meant being slimmer would make her husband want to spend more time with her. Mum wanted her life to be the same as it had been when they first moved into the house. She had been so much in love then and still felt that underneath Dad's distant behaviour, he felt the same about her.

In the early days, he would keep telling her how great she

looked. It was those compliments she wanted to hear again, hence the crazy diet and the diet pills she took. Mum believed for a while that his waning interest in her was partly because she had been pregnant for much of the time in those early years of their marriage. She felt – not that he had said it – that he was no longer paying her compliments because he didn't like the weight she had put on. She was never fat, just a little plumper then she was in photos taken in her teenage years. But then who isn't? I think now that her obsession of getting fat was more to justify why he was having an affair.

There are other things that happened in my early life that I've never forgotten either. I remember once it was early one evening and I had never heard my dad sound so angry before: he had found out about the slimming pills. That was when the worst row between them began. We three kids were just about shaking as we sat on the top of the stairs wishing they would stop.

'You're taking drugs, you stupid woman!' he was yelling.

'I'm not, they're just vitamins,' Mum pleaded with him.

'Don't lie! I know what they are – those "diet" pills are nothing but speed. You think I don't know about these things. I can't think where you got them from, seeing as they're illegal.'

None of us knew what all that meant, but we learnt more later as the family disintegrated. Mum had taken the pills to get slimmer, but he hated the drugs being in the house and, as she took them, her behaviour became increasingly volatile and erratic.

'This meal is shite,' we heard coming from the kitchen, just before there was the sound of a plate crashing onto the floor, followed by Mum screaming. Then we heard the back door slam as our father walked out.

I heard her on the phone after that row, begging Grandad for help. Later, we also found out that he knew about that affair Dad was having. They might say women gossip but it was general knowledge to all Dad's team of workers and the rumour was all around the company. Grandad was furious that Dad hadn't ended the affair when he told him to, so he told Mum that her suspicions were real. She burst into tears on the phone and he came round to calm her down and make sure we all had some dinner and got to bed without too much further drama. That was Grandad – anything to help his family.

I don't know what advice he gave my mother because he refused to discuss anything to do with her marital problems in front of us children. But whatever the advice had been, it was ignored. More screaming rows took place between our parents. More than once we heard the thud of Dad hitting her, Mum screaming back at him. Sometimes the pair of them were landing punches on each other, which was enough to send Lucy and I sobbing to our bedrooms.

That was the beginning of all our childhood happiness and security coming to an end.

5

Dad didn't know that Mum had found out about his affair with Lorraine a couple of weeks earlier. If he had, he might have worked out just why she was taking slimming pills. Lorraine, who had been a friend of hers, had a great figure, which could only have made Mum feel even worse. If only he had known, he would hardly have got angry and maybe those rows would never have happened.

I'd like to believe that, if Dad had realised what Mum knew, he would have stopped his affair with Lorraine and tried his best to make Mum feel that she was still lovely. That might have repaired some of the damage and made them close again. But none of that happened and I was the one who witnessed Mum telling him what she had found out.

I was sitting on the kitchen table having milk and biscuits when that stormy row began. I should have scuttled out, but being a curious child and puzzling at some of the words I was hearing, I just couldn't move. Mum could not control herself as she spat out her anger.

'How could you!' she yelled. 'She was a friend of mine. Not now, though. I'd like to go round and thump her.'

'Don't you dare, we'd have all the neighbours complaining!' he warned.

'*I'm* the one complaining and I've got a bloody good reason,' she snapped. 'I'll tell you now, that one more thing from you and I'll take my children and leave you. What a lying, cheating bastard you are! I'll get Dad to sack you! Even he knows, the whole of the business is talking about it.'

'Now, come on, Paula! We've three young children to look after,' he said as calmly as he could, trying to smooth things out. I don't think that he wanted Mum to leave, and he certainly didn't want to be sacked.

'Look how upset Georgia is,' said Mum as she turned to me and put her hand on my shoulder. 'I'm sorry, darling, that you had to hear all of that.'

I muttered that I was going upstairs. Just as I jumped up, I heard Dad telling her that his affair with Lorraine meant nothing.

There was a stony silence in the house for a while after that row. At least my parents were no longer shouting at each other, but the reality was they were not even speaking. It was Lucy, with her sharp little ears, who told me one day that she had heard Dad trying to get round Mum.

'The door to the kitchen was shut, so I just stood outside and listened,' she explained. 'It was Dad doing all the talking, Mum wasn't saying anything. He kept telling her that his affair was over and that he knew it was stupid of him, because he shouldn't have done it, and he promised her that he would never do anything like that again.'

'What did Mum say?'

'Nothing. She came out of the room looking vague and hardly seemed to notice me standing at the door.'

Our brother Sid heard us whispering in my bedroom and came in to join us. He, too, wanted to hear what was going on in the house. 'It's quiet now, apart from you two chatting away, isn't it? Unless one of you has been standing at doors and listening.'

'What's an affair?' I blurted out, thinking that he, being the eldest, would surely know.

'Ah, Lucy's been eavesdropping again, has she? It means Dad is seeing another woman,' he told me.

At that age I didn't really understand what that meant, which was probably just as well.

'He told her it was only a fling,' said Lucy with one of her wicked little smiles, 'and that it's not still happening.'

That was another piece of information I didn't understand. I'm not sure if Lucy really knew what those words meant either. Our brother did, though. He pulled a face and just said, 'Bad Dad.'

In return I managed to reveal something that shook them both: 'When I was in the kitchen yesterday, Mum kept saying she was going to take us and leave him if he was ever nasty to her again.'

'I hope he's not going to have a go at her again,' Sid said. 'But I don't think he will.'

We all said that we hoped that everything would be normal again. Of course, we wanted our parents to stay together and be happy so that our lives would return to how they were before all the rows started. But they didn't. I don't know exactly what happened, just that Mum moved me into Lucy's room that weekend so she could sleep in mine.

I could tell by the expression on his face that Dad was upset that she was not in their bedroom. He did try his best to be as pleasant as possible, but Mum more or less ignored him. The atmosphere in the house was more than uncomfortable. For once we were looking forward to going to school on Monday – at least we would be away from those rows. Dad told us on the Saturday that he was going out to do a job that Grandad had given him. On hearing this, Mum shot him a dark look and sniffed.

'Now, don't worry, it's not in this road. You can ask your father where it is when you see him, seeing as you don't believe anything I tell you.'

Mum glowered at him as he said goodbye. Was it coincidence that Grandad came over that day? He hugged us children and gave us all a big packet of sweets to share. He said he wanted a chat with Mum so, as it was a sunny day, how about we went out into the garden and played a bit? We didn't need much persuasion. Out we went, hoping that Grandad would help sort out our parents' problems. None of us knew what he said to Mum, but with hindsight, I'm guessing that he told her to make up for our sakes.

If he did, Mum didn't take much notice. Over the rest of that weekend, Dad was really trying to win Mum back. When he arrived home later that afternoon, he brought in a lovely bunch of flowers and a bottle of her favourite wine.

He suggested that they sent out for a takeaway, which he would go and get – 'Save you cooking and you can relax,' he said with a smile. Not that she returned the warmth, but she did agree to him getting us all a takeaway.

We sat down to eat pizzas together and Dad poured wine into Mum's glass, before filling his own. The meal with all of us sitting together wasn't too bad – I don't think Mum wanted us to get upset again. I thought maybe, after that, I would get my bedroom back, but I didn't.

We were all still hoping that everything would turn out all right and our parents would be friendly towards each other again. Sunday seemed quite peaceful and our grandparents came over. Nan brought a homemade cake with her, which we ate most of when we had tea. At least Mum and Dad were polite to each other while our grandparents were there. That made the three of us optimistic that things were getting better.

Come Monday morning, we realised that nothing had changed. In fact, everything was worse. There we were getting ready for school when we heard a huge row downstairs.

I put my fingers in my ears, as I could hardly bear hearing them. Lucy had gone pale and tears were filling her eyes – 'I can't stand this happening every day,' she said as she sat back down on her bed.

Sid knocked on our door: 'Can I come in?'

'Yes,' we both said.

'Best stay up here till they stop their shouting,' he said. I could tell he was really fed up and also worried. So, we did as he suggested as we, too, didn't want to overhear all the terrible things they were yelling at each other. It wasn't only

Sid who was fed up, Lucy and I were too. We didn't want to be late for school and we still needed to get our breakfast.

As we heard the front door slam, a sigh of relief came from all three of us. Dad was gone and we could venture downstairs.

'It's safe to go down now, girls,' Sid told us. 'Best if we don't say anything about what we heard. Let's just get breakfast and hurry off to school. We don't want to be late. OK?'

Up until I went into the kitchen, Sid's advice sounded reasonable. It was when I saw Mum that I winced – I had never seen her look the way she did then. Her face was bright pink with rage, her eyes glittering. If that was bad enough to make us feel a little shaky, what she said then was even more alarming.

'We're leaving now,' she announced. 'I want you all to go upstairs and pack all the clothes you think you'll need for a while.' And without any further explanation, she tossed a collection of large plastic bags at us. 'I'll find a couple of suitcases for you to use as well,' she added.

'But, Mum,' my brother said, 'today's a school day and we've not had breakfast yet.'

'Then make some sandwiches, Sid. And hurry up! I want us all out of this house in less than an hour. We don't have to take everything now, just sort out what clothes you'll need for a week or so. I've ordered a taxi, we're going to move into a bed-and-breakfast. It's already booked. Forget school today, you can go tomorrow. I'll give you all a note to take, explaining why you're not there today. 'Remember, you don't have to pack much. I can arrange to get everything else later.'

We were all tearful and upset.

Did Mum really think that would be a good way of getting her revenge? Right up into my teens, I wondered why she didn't just kick him out instead of us having to leave. After all, we knew Grandad had paid the deposit on the house. I suppose she wasn't thinking straight and maybe she believed that, once we moved out for a while, Dad would move out too. That might have been the reason she said not to take that much with us. Perhaps she was leaving everything for Grandad to sort out.

'I doubt he'll go nicely,' Mum said to us a couple of days later. 'But when he cools down, I'll talk to your grandad. He can tell him to leave and get the locks changed.'

But if Mum thought that was really going to happen, she got it all wrong. For a start, she should have checked whose name was on the deeds of the house. Had she done so, she would have seen that the name was the same as the person who had applied for and was paying the mortgage: Dad. Things were different then, I suppose. Her plan for revenge wasn't going to work at all.

That was the first of Mum's many bad mistakes.

6

So, that Monday morning, instead of making our way to school, we placed all our luggage into the boot of a cab. When that was full, we sat on the back seat, the rest of our smaller bags on our laps. We were quite bewildered at the enormity of having to leave and must have looked pretty miserable when the cab started moving away. Together in unison, we turned around to watch the house that we had called home disappear from sight. Each of us said our goodbyes in our own way – after all, this had been our home since we were born and we were more than sorry to be leaving it. We were also very confused by what Mum had said about why we had to do this. Lucy and I had protested a little, but Sid was far more outspoken, saying, 'It's our home, Mum – we don't want to leave it, or Dad.' His words, which Mum could see we all agreed with, made her even more angry. She just about screamed at us, 'If you want to stay with your dad, then go ahead, stay! But I'm leaving. Now get yourselves going if you want to come with me.'

'We do want to come with you, Mum,' Lucy and I told her quickly, hoping this would calm her down. We might not have wanted to leave our home or Dad, but there was no way we wanted to stay behind without Mum being there. I still think that Sid was tempted to say he would stay, but hearing us two, he kept quiet. I doubt if he wanted to be in the house on his own for a lot of the time, especially if Dad was always with Lorraine. In his own way he was fiercely loyal to Mum and us two girls. He also recognised that Mum was almost hysterical and, as I've learnt, boys don't like to see their mother or their sisters breaking down.

The journey seemed to take a while. We passed shops, small houses and a tired-looking cinema, none of which we recognised. When we suddenly turned into another road, I heard the driver say, 'It's about halfway down here.'

'So that's where we're staying?' Lucy whispered in my ear as we passed row upon row of red-brick terraced houses, many of them turned into flats.

The cab pulled up in front of a large house. I had thought we must be going to a small hotel but this house, with its neon sign in one of the ground-floor windows, told us that it was a B&B. There was a cardboard sign on a string that said 'No vacancies'.

'It's really grim, isn't it?' Lucy whispered. 'Just look at those windows, they all need cleaning!'

I'm guessing the driver thought the same as us. I could see he looked rather puzzled. After all, he had picked us up from a smart-looking detached house in quite a well-off area. He must have been wondering why he was taking us somewhere like this, in such a dilapidated street. As he helped us get our luggage out of the boot and took it to the front door, he was tactful enough not to offer an opinion, though.

Mum slipped the fare money to him and gave him an extra tip for helping us.

'Thank you, Mam, and good luck,' he told her before getting into his cab and driving off. I'm sure I'm not imagining this, but to me, he looked a bit sad.

If we hadn't been impressed by the house, we didn't think much of the landlady either. Mum rang the bell and a grey-haired woman wearing a creased and stained skirt with a long baggy jumper opened the door and ushered us in. There was no friendly greeting, not even a smile, just, 'I'll take you up to your rooms,' as she pointed to the staircase. Maybe it was because Mum was looking pretty smart that no warmth came from her, or perhaps she didn't like youngsters in her house. Either way, as we pulled our cases to the staircase, I heard her mutter to Mum, 'Your children are not to play on the stairs or in the dining room.'

She led the way up the stairs and I just about caught my breath when she opened the door to our room. I was used to comfortable, clean bedrooms. This one had a small double and a single bed crammed inside. I was very young then, but I'm convinced that what we smelt was damp. As for the bedding, it was a mix of old, yellowish and very thin, un-ironed sheets and faded blankets – nothing like our bedding at home. I just hoped at least it was clean.

Sid took his bag into the room right next to ours. It didn't take him long to come back out with a scowl on his face.

'It's like a nasty cupboard,' he said, 'I can hardly turn round and the bed's horrible, all hard and lumpy.'

'We're not going to be here for long,' Mum told him. 'I've 'booked another place for us in a couple of days.'

'Why's that?' he asked.

'Because this one's fully booked next week.'

'I think Mum's lost her marbles,' said Sid when the three of us were alone for a short while. 'Bet the next place is no better than this. Can hardly be much worse, though.'

'I hope not! I don't like this place and, as for that landlady, I don't want to be anywhere near her ...' Lucy stopped moaning as soon as Mum came back into our room. She told us that she was taking us out for lunch. After having hardly any breakfast, it took us just five minutes to get ready to go out. I don't think us three were expecting the sort of cafe we went into after a short walk from the house – I'd never been in a little place like that before. Still, the food was nice enough, even if we were sat at Formica tables where the smell of fryer oil mingled with cigarette smoke.

When we had finished our meal, Mum did a bit of shopping so that we could make sandwiches in our room. In both the shop and the cafe, I had heard Mum's mobile ring, but she just ignored it – she didn't even look to see who it was. She must have known that it was either Dad or her father and that neither of them would be very pleased with what she had done. Maybe she didn't feel ready to explain anything to either of them.

We spent the rest of the day in our rooms, which made me miss our home even more. There was no music to listen to, no television to watch and no garden to go outside and play in.

Lucy and I didn't mind sharing a bedroom, but as much as we loved our mum, we didn't like spending the night in the same room as her. We could hardly chat to each other and we had loads of things we wanted to talk about because the whole situation was so confusing for us. Not only did Mum keep her bedside light on very late, which made it hard to sleep, but even when she switched it off, she was restless. She must have had some scary dreams because she kept calling out in her sleep, which constantly woke us up.

We wanted to brush our teeth and wash before bed as well as in the morning. Being girls, having to use a communal bathroom bothered us. That first night we went off with our towels over our arms and a small toilet bag with our toothbrushes, toothpaste as well as two flannels and a bar of soap inside. We were disappointed when we saw the bathroom door was shut and we could hear taps running. Then we noticed someone in a dressing gown making her way there to have a bath.

'Guess we'll have to make do with the little basin in our room,' Lucy said. Another reason to miss our home with its pretty pink-tiled bathroom.

As for the toilet, it was horrid. The seat was always up and it had thin, cheap toilet paper. Not everyone left it clean either.

All these years later, none of us have forgotten the breakfasts that were put in front of us. We reckoned our landlady must have been an insomniac who crawled out of bed at dawn to cook all the breakfasts. Cold, fatty bacon with a couple of eggs that, having been fried ages ago, had ended up as hard yellow-and-white lumps. At least the toast was freshly made because the toaster was on the sideboard for us to operate ourselves. There was cheap margarine, full of other people's toast crumbs, and the jam was thin and runny. As for cereal, it must have been in those boxes for months – it was so stale and hard, like eating dried cardboard, despite the milk we added to it. I really don't know how we managed to swallow any of it. Probably because for once, we could hardly wait to go to school.

Before she took us to the bus stop, Mum handed us an envelope to give to the headteacher. She explained that it contained a letter, telling him why we had missed a day of school.

When I look back at that time today, my memory is a bit fuzzy. I guess I tried to forget how bad it was. All I know is that we stayed in several places, some better and some worse, but I can't remember much about them, only that we never liked them. Moving around meant we had to keep catching different buses to get to and from school. That hardly made those weekdays easy, especially if we had moved in the middle of that week.

We all wanted a home, with our own bedrooms. Not only that, but we also missed meeting up with our friends. We couldn't even tell them where we were staying as Mum had warned us not to say anything. Besides, their parents wouldn't want them catching buses to and fro to the area we were staying in.

Hearing our moans one morning, Mum told us she had finally found a place where we would have our own rooms – 'And there's a bed settee in the living room, which I can sleep on.'

'What sort of house is it?' Lucy asked suspiciously.

'It's a flat and we move in on Saturday,' said Mum.

We all felt pretty relieved that we were at least moving into somewhere more permanent. It had to be nicer than the grubby B&Bs we'd been staying in. Or so we thought, until we arrived there. If someone asked me to describe it, all I can say is that it was beyond shabby. Lucy called it a disgusting slum and nearly burst into tears. Sid kept silent, but I could see from his face that he thought it was awful too. Every inch of it needed cleaning. I suppose we should have guessed that we weren't going to a place that was any great shakes when we were driven there. All the flats and little houses looked pretty uncared for.

As we went in, Mum told us to go straight to our rooms with our stuff – the small entranceway was already so cluttered. We unpacked and managed to hang some of our clothes up on a hook at the back of the bedroom door. There was a small chest of drawers, but no wardrobe and Lucy complained about the carpet: 'Look at it! It's got stains all over it and it smells of wet dog.' She was right, of course, but there was nothing to be done and Mum seemed to be turning a blind eye to her complaints.

It was when we were looking around the rest of the flat and went into the sitting room with its sagging settee that Lucy noticed there were earwigs on the carpet. She shot back to our bedroom and found there were some in our room as well. That scared her: 'Mum, they could get into our ears when we're sleeping!'

'It's only a myth that they eat your brains when they get inside your ear,' Sid told her with a wry smile. 'We did that in biology.'

'I promise we'll get that sorted, Lucy,' Mum told her firmly.

A little later, while Lucy and Sid were doing their best to clean the kitchen, I was checking each drawer in the chest of drawers with suspicion as I put socks and underwear into them.

Then Mum called us all into the sitting room: 'Nan's coming over on Monday.' We guessed that she must have finally asked her parents for help and we were delighted when she told us that Nan would still be there when we got home from school. 'She wants to see all of you so please don't moan about this place too much. I promise she'll help me get it looking better. And before you ask, Lucy, she'll know what to do about the earwigs. I'm sure she'll know how to deal with them or else she'll get someone in.'

'Is Grandad coming too?' I asked.

'No, he's very busy right now,' Mum answered but I saw her face drop a little when I asked that.

For once we all hurried home from school and, racing to the stop, we caught the earlier bus just in time. When we went in, Nan beamed at us and there were hugs all round. She had brought some groceries over and one of her wonderful homemade fruit cakes. When Mum was out of the room, Lucy told her about the earwigs.

'I know, dear, your mother told me. I'm going to get your grandad to send a couple of workmen over right away. They'll get rid of them and clean all the stains off the carpets as well. You'll be able to sleep better then, won't you, Lucy?'

We were much happier, although we wished Grandad would come over himself. I didn't understand then, but I did a few years later, why he wasn't pleased with his daughter. It was clearly for our sakes that he sent a couple of his workmen over the following day while we were at school. When we came back and walked into the flat, we could tell immediately that it smelt fresher.

When I was a little older, I learnt that the whole catalogue of problems Mum had had landed on Grandad's shoulders. Or should I say the mistakes she made without thinking that they might have implications for the whole of our family. Little wonder Grandad kept away from her for a while. That day, when she told us we were leaving, she thought that he would take her side and boot Dad out of the house. Her wish fell apart when Grandad found out that the house had been registered in his son-in-law's name alone. He was furious, especially as he had provided the deposit and funded many of the improvements. If that wasn't bad enough, behind everyone's back, Dad sold the house very quickly. He refused to have an estate agent's sign outside because he didn't want Grandad or any of his workmen to see it.

I can't help thinking that he might have triggered that last row with Mum so that she would leave. In a way I can hardly blame him, for he must have concluded by then that their marriage was over. On the other hand, I still feel disappointed that he kept the deposit that Grandad had put up, as well as all the profit on the sale. The value of the house had increased by thousands over the years he and Mum had lived there. His excuse was that he couldn't find himself both broke and jobless. Anyway, he had put in many hours of his own labour to transform the house. Grandad said he didn't need to leave the firm as he was a good worker so that excuse didn't hold water, but at least he had packed up some of our belongings. He left them with the purchaser, who rang Grandad up to ask for them to be collected.

It was that phone call that told Grandad what his son-in-law had done and he was furious at being cheated in such a devious way. Had he known about the house being up for sale, he would have asked for his deposit back and made him give Mum half the profit on the house, which was probably the reason my dad had sold it so craftily. He was also angry with his daughter for signing papers putting the house in Dad's name alone without seeking advice from him or his lawyer. If Mum had gone to a solicitor or even to her parents when she decided to leave, she would have been told that she and her three children must stay in the house. It was Dad who would have been made to leave, not her. The fact that he had been repeatedly unfaithful would have been a good enough reason for her to want him out of the family home. Grandad's large deposit meant that the monthly mortgage repayments had been quite low because he had wanted to give his daughter financial security. It's a wonder my father wasn't taken to court, but I suppose Grandad didn't want to cause any more upset for his grandchildren. Of course, the moment the house was sold for a good price, Dad stopped working for Grandad and disappeared for a while.

It was just not long enough.

7

During the months we lived in that flat, Nan, who did her best to hide her annoyance at her three grandchildren living in those circumstances, was a regular visitor. She always brought something for all of us when she came, such as homemade cakes and books. 'Reading,' she told us, 'is good for you. It's food for the brain.'

'We'd better get stuck in then,' Sid would say each time she left.

We were aware that questions about the content of those books would be asked on the next visit. This was Nan's way of widening our general knowledge. Luckily, she knew us all well enough to know what sort of books we liked.

As well as visiting during the week, Nan would take us out on two Saturdays a month for afternoon tea. We all enjoyed those occasions even more. Mum made herself look as good as possible – her hair washed and blow-dried, before she put on a clean, well-ironed outfit. She was still youthful and lovely then. While she was getting ready, Lucy and I brushed each other's hair and made sure we, too, looked neat and tidy. As for Sid, somehow our brother had a knack of always looking like that.

Nan would arrive bang on time, give one ring of the bell and wait for us outside by her car. I think not having to go into the flat was a relief for her. The three of us were bundled into the back while Mum sat comfortably in the front as Nan drove the few miles to a much better area and the charming tearoom that we all liked.

The owners, who were a married couple, were always welcoming and they certainly offered a wonderful afternoon tea. Savoury thin sandwiches without crusts, freshly baked scones with jam and cream, and a choice of cake. My favourite was always two huge pink meringues sandwiched with cream. Lucy liked the carrot cake and Sid loved the Black Forest gateau. Talk about feeling full up when we left! Even Mum, who always seemed to be dieting, did not turn those fluffy scones down.

There was another visit from Nan that still stands out in my memory. She had gone to see Mum while we were at school – I suppose she must have wanted to talk to her daughter about something important when we were not there.

Evidently, Dad had packed some of our belongings that we had left behind. Nan had brought the ones she decided we might need. She wanted to know if Mum had room for some of the other boxes too. The crockery had been put in large boxes and there were pans and bed linen too.

'Now, do you want all that brought over?' she asked. 'I don't think the crockery and more pans will be much good in this tiny kitchen.'

When we arrived home from school, Nan told us that she had all the clothes we left behind – 'Though I'm sure you must have outgrown some of them. I can see you've shot up a bit, Lucy, and Sid, I doubt these shoes still fit you.'

'If my clothes are too small, then Georgia might like them,' my sister said, giggling as she nudged me in the ribs.

The one thing that pleased us more than having all our familiar clothes back to sort through was the prospect of going to sleep under our lovely, familiar bedding. Having that on our beds would be so much better than the sheets that came with the flat, which were even worse than some of the B&B ones.

Nothing was said to us about Dad that day, although Mum knew by then what he had been up to. Neither of our grandparents wanted us to hear that he had sold the house and pocketed all the money, even though, strictly speaking, it was not all his. He had also allowed the buyers to have all the furniture, the fridge, the washing machine and other household gadgets. Our grandparents must have decided that we were too young to know the depth of his betrayal.

When Nan heard us saying we might go to the house to see him, she was forced to tell us that he had moved out.

'Where's he gone?' we piped up.

'Not sure, darlings, but I expect he'll be in touch with you soon,' came the reply before she quickly tried to change the subject.

I'm sure that Nan could tell by our expressions that the three of us were hoping that we could go back to the house we still thought of as home. Sid was the one who would not just accept this and he was determined to find out why we weren't moving back in if Dad had left. Immediately he began to ask more questions, but Nan covered up by saying he had some people staying there for a while.

We found out some of the truth a little later. It wasn't Nan who told us how Dad had sold the house and all its contents, it was Mum's sister, Aunty Clare. She was tactful enough not to tell us just what else he had done, such as keeping Grandad's deposit and a few other unpleasant things. The main reason she felt she had to tell us was because Nan was worried that we might go round to the house and ask when our dad was coming back and could we have his phone number.

'It's best not to tell your mum that I've explained a few things to you,' said Clare. 'She and your dad have to sort a few things out when they're ready so best if you don't ask her any more questions. I know it's not been easy for her. Your nan has told you that he'll get in touch with you all in a while, hasn't she?'

'Yes, but how long do you think that will be?' Sid persisted, although it was me who was actually the one who missed Dad the most.

'I don't know, but I doubt it'll be long.'

What Clare had been told was that Dad had already contacted his in-laws by letter. In it, he mentioned that he wanted to see his children, pointing out that he had every right to. He complained that Mum had never left her address for him so he didn't know where we were. Of course, he could go up to the school and wait for us, but that was not the way he wanted to do it.

In other words, he believed that Grandad would have one of his men who Dad didn't know looking out for him at the school gates. In a way, him only giving Grandad a post-office address in another county was proof indeed that he was nervous of him and that's why he never gave a physical address. After all, Grandad had friends who mixed in criminal circles and, if he was angry enough, he could cause Dad a huge problem. Yes, Dad probably did want to see us, but not enough to potentially risk his life.

I found out a long time later that Grandad had replied saying he was more than angry and it would be better for Dad to stay away until he felt a little calmer.

8

About two or three days after Nan's visit, a new fridge and a washing machine were delivered. Mum said Nan had phoned her to make sure she would be in when they came. We came home from school and saw the new appliances in the kitchen – 'Your grandmother said they're here because you three needed them.'

That made us laugh.

'It's so good of her,' she kept saying, genuinely grateful.

I had heard her asking about Grandad the first couple of times when Nan came over. The excuse that he was busy was the one she always used in front of us. I'm sure she would have explained the real reason to Mum when we were not around. By the look on her face when she heard Nan's excuse, I knew Mum was disappointed that her dad had not forgiven her.

It must have been getting on for a year after we had left the house that Grandad decided to visit his daughter. Mum knew he had met us after school quite a few times and she was upset by it, especially when she heard he had taken us to a cafe and then put us in a taxi to get home, rather than bring us himself. That made us feel a little guilty, but there was nothing we could do about it – we were still children after all.

None of us knew that Grandad was going to come over to see her. When she told us about his visit, she was just so happy. She said that everything had been made up between them, not that she mentioned what their problem had been.

It was the following Monday when Grandad met us from school again. Only this time he was not going to take us to a cafe, instead he was taking us home – 'I've got something I want to tell your mum and I want you all to hear it too,' was all he told us, but it was enough to make us deadly curious. Lucy must have been biting her lips to stop her asking what it was – she was always the nosy one out of us three.

Mum looked really surprised when the four of us turned up together. She was so pleased to see her father again so soon after their last meeting, especially when he gave her a hug and said, 'Let's sit down – we can get some tea in five minutes, but I want to tell you all something first.'

It barely took more than a couple of minutes before our faces were pink with excitement.

'Your mother was right,' he said, looking at Mum. 'She hated the fact that you were all living here, she thought it wasn't good for you three either,' he added, looking over at us children with a smile. 'The school's too far away for you, isn't it?'

'It is a bit,' noted Sid, to which we all nodded in agreement.

'It means you can't be around your friends, doesn't it?

The bus takes time to get here and your nan and I wouldn't like to think of you walking down this road when the evenings get dark.'

'No, Grandad,' we said.

'That's why I always put you in a taxi when we meet. Well, I thought about how your life has changed and I've seen how you're all making the best of it. No complaints from any of you. It's that which has made me find a three-bedroom house for you all to move into. It's not far from the school either, which will make life easier.'

Mum just about gasped when he told us that and her eyes started to well with tears. As for us three, we were almost jumping with joy and rushed to hug Grandad.

'My workmen are decorating it now. When that's done, new carpets will be going down. No earwigs for you to worry about, young Lucy! Your mother's sorting out furniture and it's all going to be delivered on Friday. All being well, you can move in over the weekend. I'll send a truck with a couple of my men so that everything you need can be put in it, including the new washing machine and the fridge your mother's already given you.'

Now Mum was grinning from ear to ear, happy at the thought of getting out of the flat. 'We'll get everything sorted by Saturday morning, first thing, Dad, and thank you, thank you so very much,' she told him shakily. This time it was she who got up and hugged him. 'Can't tell you how grateful I am,' she added, brushing away another tear.

He just patted her on the shoulder and said, 'I know you are, darling.'

Grandad must have seen how thrilled us three were – we could hardly sit still, we were so happy. How we had hated that pokey flat.

'I'd better get us all some tea and some of Nan's fruit cake to celebrate,' she told him as she walked over to the kitchen, with Lucy following to help.

Now we would be able to invite friends over; life would be like it used to be.

Over the coming week, we each packed up our own clothes and books, as well as a few other things we had accumulated into those well-used cases and bags.

'I bet Nan's already got the place perfect,' Lucy said as Sid joined us in our room before bedtime on our last night in the flat.

'Mum won't have to sleep on that horrid settee that turns into a bed any more. That should please her, she'll have her own bedroom again,' he said.

'No more screaming rows coming from it either!' Lucy giggled.

*   *   *

Lucy and I woke at the crack of dawn on the morning we were leaving.

'I can't wait to get out of here!' my sister said each time another bag was put in the hall, ready to be loaded into the truck.

'Me too,' I told her.

I don't think any of us could believe that Grandad had done this for us.

On the day of the move, we all got up really early. Mum made breakfast and, once we had finished it, we looked around one last time to make sure nothing of ours was left behind. We then waited for the truck to arrive at ten o'clock, which was the time we had been told.

Grandad's two men took everything out for us, including all our suitcases and plastic bags stuffed full of clothes, towels and bedding.

As we climbed into the truck, we could hardly wait to see our new home. Not only was it near to school, but it was in a much better area. Sid was beaming from ear to ear.

Mum turned round when we reached a road she recognised and told us that she thought we were nearly there. Minutes later, the truck pulled up in the driveway of a red-brick semi-detached house.

'This must be our new home,' she said with a note of amazement in her voice.

Dying to see inside, we all clambered out of the truck as fast we could and raced to the front door.

The moment we stepped through the door that Nan held open, we were overjoyed by what we saw. Not only did the place look clean, with its cream walls and brand-new biscuit coloured fitted carpets, it also smelt of fresh paint and the woollen smell of new carpets. As for the furniture, Nan had chosen well: there was a long pale-blue settee in the living room, a couple of comfy armchairs and a light-oak bookcase. She had even found some paintings to go on the walls and there was a vase of flowers on the coffee table.

While the men took in the washing machine and fridge,

Sid helped with the cases. They stayed on to plumb everything in and we all thanked them when they left. Sid was keen to see his bedroom, as were Lucy and I. Nan had certainly been generous – we had brand-new pillows and duvets, a fitted wardrobe each, as well as a chest of drawers and two small sets of drawers by the side of our beds.

Sid came knocking on our door: 'Nan's even put a desk in mine, with a reading lamp so I can do homework!' he told us. I could see how excited he was. 'It's great being here, isn't it?' he added.

That's what we all thought. We believed that now our lives were going to be so much better. Sadly, that belief did not last for very long.

9

It was in that house where, within just a few months, our childhoods were to become unbearable. During the few years we were to stay there, my mind began to take almost photographic images of our distress and filed them away in my memory. It's as if they're in a photograph album that's so hard to look at, I want to keep it tightly shut. But even now, after all these years, it springs open in my mind, forcing me to face those pictures from my past.

At the beginning, the three of us really appreciated Grandad buying us our new home. We simply loved being there and we all believed that living in that house with its lovely fresh look and all the new furniture was going to provide the perfect home for us. Mum appeared to feel exactly the same, which really pleased us. She kept it bright and clean and made sure that she was up before us on the mornings we went to school so that she could make us a good breakfast. In the afternoon when we returned, the aroma of freshly baked cakes wafted from the kitchen. They were part of our afternoon snack when we arrived back. Mum would sit down with us at the table and ask how our day had gone.

How I wish she had stayed that way – but she didn't.

In those early weeks she seemed really happy and lively. It took about a month for us to notice tiny changes in her. Had we all been a few years older then, not only would we have spotted certain signs sooner, but we might also have worked out what was causing them.

It was Lucy who first noticed that Mum's pupils were often constricted – 'It's like they keep going small and that can't be right, can it? I really hope it's not a problem with her eyesight.' My sister's face was more puzzled than concerned, appealing to Sid and I to help her understand what was happening.

Then there were other things about Mum that, young as I was, I couldn't help noticing, such as her face often being flushed in the afternoon. There were times when she would give us a wide smile and chatter almost nonstop, but when we three quizzed each other when we were out of her earshot, none of us thought that what she had said was making much sense.

I was the one who asked the others if they thought it was possible that Mum had had a couple of drinks while waiting for us to get home from school. After all, she and Dad had often had wine with their dinner and so we knew that Mum could get a bit silly after a drink or two.

'Don't know, though she does gabble a bit – it's just a bit weird,' was Sid's view, but when I asked Lucy what she thought, she pointed out that there were no bottles of alcohol in the house.

'She doesn't smell of it either, does she, Georgia?' she said to me when we were in our bedroom. 'Maybe she chatters a lot because she's been on her own all day.'

A week or so later, Lucy – who must had been thinking about what I had said – took me to one side: 'I think she's back on those slimming pills again. Don't you remember how weird she seemed then and how angry Dad got? Those rows were terrible, weren't they?'

'They happened all the time,' I said. 'When I'd gone to bed, I could still hear them – I used to put my hands over my ears. I hated hearing Mum scream at Dad and him shouting back at her. It was really horrible. Even when they stopped, I still couldn't get back to sleep for ages.'

'It gave you bad nightmares as well, didn't it? They used to wake me up,' my sister said.

'Yes, I know you would get out of bed and try to calm me and sometimes came into bed with me.'

'I think Dad threw away all those pills of hers. That was one of the reasons why they rowed – he didn't want them in the house,' Lucy told me. 'He kept calling them "speed", whatever that means. But I bet she's managed to get some more now.'

'A tablet called "speed" sounds a bit stupid. What do you think it is?'

'I don't know,' Lucy replied, 'but you could try asking Sid – he always seems to know a lot.'

At this, we both giggled. Sid could sometimes be a bit of know-it-all when it came to his sisters.

Sid told Lucy that those little tablets called 'speed' would stop Mum feeling hungry or tired and make her walk faster, which would then also help her become slimmer. Having learnt more about them, none of us thought that taking them was a good idea. What none of us realised was that Mum's drug habit was beginning to spiral out of control. Later, we would discover that she was already taking something much stronger than speed. Strong enough for her to appear quite unwell when she was coming down from whatever it was.

At this point in our lives only Sid, who was after all the eldest, knew a little about the danger of drugs. Neither Lucy nor I had any idea of the damage they could cause. The schools were doing their best to try to make students understand the reasons for not taking them, whereas us three were receiving our own salutary lessons at home.

By the time I was nine and Lucy was twelve, we had seen things that young children should never have seen. We knew what syringes were used for and, more than that, we saw the people who came to the house just push up their sleeves and then help each other pull the rubber band tightly around the part of their arms above their elbows, which made their veins bulge. It was then that the syringes, already laden with heated liquid, appeared in their hands. Sickened, we tried to turn our heads away so that we didn't see those needles going into the veins. We hated how these people just flopped over until the drug hit them; we wanted them to leave Mum alone and stop coming, but there was nothing we could do.

The only good thing about that time was that, although we were much too young to receive those lessons, they frightened me enough so that, even now, I hardly let myself take an aspirin.

10

There were a few more steps to take before we all had to admit that there was something very wrong going on in our home. I'm sure Sid became instantly suspicious when we returned from school to find Mum dozing on the settee. Lucy and I just thought she must have caught some bug or was just very tired, but I don't think our brother did.

For the first few times she was like that, she woke quite easily. Her excuses about being tired and needing an afternoon nap convinced Lucy and I that this explanation was fairly genuine. However, the day came within a short time when none of us believed her. It was a Friday afternoon when Sid had stayed on at school to play football and Lucy and I came home together to find her sprawled on the settee. Lucy did her best to wake her, which took a while. Mum's eyes were bleary when she opened them and she was obviously struggling to sit up and kept falling back onto the cushions.

'Come on, Mum, let me help you,' Lucy told her. 'I'll put a cushion behind you.' Placing her arms around Mum's shoulders, she managed to get her sitting up. It was as if her muscles couldn't support her weight, even when seated. 'I'll make you a cup of tea, shall I?'

'Oh, thank you, Lucy. That would be lovely – I don't know why I'm feeling so tired ...'

Nor did we – not then.

If our mum being like that had only happened once, more than likely we would have forgotten about it, but these episodes began to occur quite frequently. Lucy and I began to dread getting home, especially if Sid wasn't with us. Each time we wondered how Mum was going to be when we got there. But Sid was with us on one of those days when we walked in and found her sound asleep. As usual, it was Lucy who woke her up. Mum's eyes opened and we all heard those feeble excuses such as feeling tired or having a headache and a few of the others that had joined her repertoire as well.

Sid gave a look that must have told her he didn't believe any of it. Although he loved his mother, he couldn't stand seeing her lying around looking so dishevelled with her smudged make-up and messy hair.

'I'll get you a cup of tea, Mum,' Lucy said, as she always did.

'I'll let you two sort her out,' said Sid. 'I've got homework to do so I'm going up to my bedroom.'

Those were the words he used every time he wanted to escape the scene downstairs. Sid's excuse was used again and again but, as he disappeared into his room, we could tell he was worried.

By now it had become almost a daily occurrence and we had all got to a point where we felt we couldn't stand it any longer. She was beginning to be a different mother from the one we had known since we were babies. One particular day, she lay slumped sideways, her face was pale, her eyes tightly shut, and her breathing sounded heavy to us.

'That's not an afternoon nap,' Sid had said when he saw her. 'I don't think she's going to wake up for a while. Lucy, please don't look so worried.'

As the tears streamed down her face, Lucy looked more than worried – she was just about defeated, I thought. Sid and I could hear her saying, 'Are you asleep, Mum?' For once, Sid stayed with us. I could tell he was concerned about Lucy as her voice became shriller when she kept on pleading, 'Wake up, Mum.' She had leant down a little and was trying to gently shake her: 'Mum, come on, please. Please, Mum.'

We all knew then that this time there was something very wrong: she wasn't just asleep.

'If she doesn't wake soon, we'll have to ring Nan, won't we?' Lucy said, a look of fear in her eyes.

No sooner had she said this than there was a collected sigh of relief as Mum's eyes opened. She looked up at Lucy and said, 'Hello, darling.' Just as Sid and I moved a little closer, those big blue eyes of hers closed again, her head dropped and her deep breathing continued.

'Oh, just let her sleep it off – she'll wake up later,' Sid sighed. 'Let's go into the kitchen and get ourselves something to eat. Don't think she'll be getting us our dinner today and I could do with a sandwich to keep me going. Got a pile of homework to do.'

'All right,' said Lucy, 'let's go into the kitchen and see what we can find.'

As we walked in, Lucy gasped, 'Oh no, just look at the kitchen! It's a right mess.' For the first time, I heard her sound annoyed about Mum. 'She's done nothing today, just left it for us to clean up and all of us have homework to do as well – it's not just you, Sid,' she added indignantly.

It certainly was a grubby mess. The washing up was piled up from the day before, as well as our breakfast plates. There were several glasses on the grimy work surfaces and, when we popped a few things in the bin, we spotted a couple of empty bottles. Was drinking the reason that Mum was just about out of it all of the time? It looked as if she had drunk the lot and kept pouring it into different glasses – that would have made her a bit more than dozy, wouldn't it?

It was then that I noticed several empty beer bottles in one of the corners of the kitchen. I pointed them out and the others looked.

'Mum doesn't ever drink beer, even on a hot day,' Lucy said, and we all knew that was true. 'Looks like she's had visitors. I wonder who they were,' Lucy said, looking a bit puzzled. 'I'll ask her when she's awake. Maybe she's making friends in the area. Anyway, let's get the washing up done, Georgia, and Sid, can you take out the rubbish bin and all those empty beer bottles?'

'Sure,' said Sid.

But it wasn't picking up the bottles or taking out the rubbish that concerned Sid, it was finding a syringe that had been recently used in the bin outside. At the time he didn't mention it to Lucy and I because he was a good older brother who didn't want to worry his sisters. Instead, he helped us by putting some of the clean crockery away.

Once we were all satisfied that the kitchen was squeaky clean again, we went through the fridge to see what we could eat for dinner.

'There are plenty of eggs, about ten of them, and some cheese,' Lucy told us with her head still in the fridge. 'Good thing Nan showed me how to make omelettes. We can have them. Anyone want a ham sandwich and a yogurt now before we start our homework?'

'Good idea. I'll get going on mine straight after – loads to do today as well,' said Sid. 'We can do our homework in our rooms and leave Mum where she is – she'll probably wake up in a while.'

He tiptoed into the living room with us following him quietly to pick up our satchels. All this time Mum had not moved.

Once homework was finished, we came and had another look at Mum. She had altered her position a little, which made us hope that she was waking up. Her eyes fluttered and a small smile crept onto her face. Lucy did what she always did and brought her in some tea, while Sid and I laid the table. That night Lucy cooked really good cheese omelettes for all of us and gave Mum her dinner on a tray so that she didn't need to get up. When she had finished, Mum told us she needed an early night and slowly walked to her bedroom in a dreamlike state, leaving us to clear up again.

That was the first inkling of us always having to clean the house and prepare meals. Not an easy life for girls of eight and ten but, somehow, we managed – at least for another two years.

When the three of us walked into the kitchen the next morning, there was no sign of breakfast being cooked, nor any hint of Mum having been up.

'She must still be asleep, I suppose,' said Sid, 'although she always has her alarm set so she can do breakfast.'

As there wasn't much time before we had to leave for school, we raided the fridge, looking for something we could put in a quick sandwich. There was still a small wedge of cheese left and Lucy quickly got out the bread and made us a sandwich each. We didn't even bother sitting down, just stood up, ate it quickly, before grabbing our satchels and heading off to school.

We didn't say much on our way there. None of us were in good spirits, our minds too full of Mum's problems – or at least the ones she had begun to place on our young shoulders.

I don't know whether Sid was dreading going home as much as Lucy and I were. When we went into the playground during our breaks Lucy would come over to talk to me.

We shared the same concerns about whether Mum would be in the same state as she had been the day before.

When school finished for the day, we were on tenterhooks as we began to walk back. Sid had something on so he would be home a bit later. Lucy looked stressed and, from the moment we left the school gates, I felt butterflies fluttering away in my stomach.

When we opened the door and walked in, I was just about holding my breath, waiting to hear Mum calling out to us. Relief brushed away all our anxieties when we saw her. No semi-conscious sprawling on the settee, instead she was looking like the mum we all loved. There was a warm smile on her face, her hair that fell to her shoulders was back to being shiny and freshly shampooed and she was wearing a crisp white shirt and a pair of pale-blue trousers, neither of which were in the least bit crumpled. She must have showered and made a real effort for us and, as we went into the kitchen, it was evident that a lot of housework must have occurred while we were out. In the scrupulously clean kitchen, still smelling of bleach and detergent, we saw that the fridge was full and a simmering casserole was on the stove.

After our homework was finished and dinner was ready, we all sat down together. Mum kept her chatter up, only this time it was coherent and interesting. She asked a few questions about school and then told us something that made us all feel excited.

'Grandad's getting me a car! He came round when I was vacuuming so I had to leave it. As we were having tea and biscuits, he told me all about it. He said a car would make bringing back the shopping much easier, and now Sid is doing more after school, we can go and pick him up too. As for weekends, I'll be able to take you all out. What do you think about that?'

'That's great, Mum,' we told her, smiling gleefully. There were lots of places that we wanted to go to in the area and it would be fun to get out of the city at weekends. By the time we went to bed, we were a lot more cheerful than we had been for a couple of days.

Over the next few days, we all fell into the trap of assuming that Mum, for the sake of her family, had completely sorted herself out. Only Sid knew about the syringe at that time. He was trying to protect his younger sisters from knowing about that. He kept quiet, but he later confessed that he was almost convinced that it belonged to whoever it was who had drunk the beer. We were all so pleased with how she had changed back into the mum we loved that we never asked her who the visitors had been.

I'm not saying that she didn't try to stay like that – I think she regretted for a long time that she was unable to be the mother we all deserved. The sad part about all of this is that she only managed to give us the impression that she was back to being the mother we loved for a total of ten days. During that time the house remained tidy, our dinners were on the hob when we came home from school, and Mum's good humour had us all enjoying sitting together at the table and talking about what each of us had done that day.

It was on the eleventh day, which was a Saturday, that our doubts about her began again. Lucy refused to contemplate that she had slipped back – 'She seems tired, but I think she's just got a cold coming,' she kept saying. She pointed out that Mum had watery eyes and there was the constant wiping of her nose. I agreed with this diagnosis, although Sid looked stern and said nothing.

It was when she was wrapped up in her dressing gown that I noticed that she had become a little thinner and her hair was no longer shiny. On learning that Mum had a cold and was not feeling very well, Nan insisted on coming over. With her astute gaze, she might have seen it wasn't a cold Mum had, but something that she would be very concerned about.

I could hear Mum on the phone giving Nan all the excuses: that she didn't want her to catch a cold or, worse still, the flu. Sid was also listening and I saw his eyebrows raise a bit at her protests.

Nan being Nan, she told her that she would bring some food over later so that she didn't have to cook and she'd better not sit too close to us children either.

'You stay here on the sofa,' Lucy told Mum. 'I heard you say that Nan's bringing over some food later – I'll just get us all a snack for now.'

Mum smiled at her as she tucked her feet up on the settee and rested her head on a cushion.

'Thank you, darling,' she said just before her eyes shut and she appeared to fall asleep.

'I don't think we'll be going out in the car this weekend,' Sid observed. And he was right. In fact, despite all the plans, we were hardly ever to travel in it together. We were all rather disappointed that first weekend as we had been so looking forward to going out. We had only been in the car once on the day when Grandad brought it over and, as Mum had to drive him home, she thought she might as well collect us all from school.

Later that day, Nan arrived with a large bag full of food and a still-warm casserole dish wrapped in foil. Lucy and I carried everything into the kitchen, while Nan went into the living room and spent a little time alone with Mum. When she left, she told Mum to take it easy and that she hoped she would be better soon.

Over the rest of the weekend, Mum just seemed tired. I helped Lucy getting our lunch and dinner ready and, as Mum remained on the sofa, it was only the three of us again who sat at the table to eat. Out of the corner of my eye, I saw her get up and totter to the door on unsteady legs before calling out that she was having another early night.

Sid's eyes followed her and, although he said nothing about what he thought then, we could tell there must be something going on in his mind that he didn't want to share.

Of course, there continued to be more excuses, such as headaches, oncoming flu and nausea. We girls were sympathetic, but Sid either rolled his eyes or headed upstairs to do homework. Maybe if we were older and more experienced, we would also have worked out that she was hardly ever telling us the truth. When Mum knew Nan was due to come over, the kitchen was clean and so was she. Showered, fully made up and the clothes she wore were spotless. She had started not to care anymore about her appearance and her clothes were often stained and her body and hair remained unwashed for days. Once Nan's visit was over, the house was once again filthy within a short time, despite everything that Lucy and I tried to do after school. It upset all of us and by then Nan too, because she wasn't stupid – she could see that both Mum and our home were going downhill.

* * *

I can remember the day that the three of us found out the real truth about how Mum was living. It was as if my mind's camera photographed much of it, so even now, nearly 30 years later, I close my eyes and see such vivid pictures of what happened. It was when we all gave up hope that Mum would change and be the mother we grew up with. Now there are times when I'm alone and, occasionally, I allow my mind to bring back the images of those days.

There's one picture that keeps coming back. It's of the people who the three of us met for the first time. None of us, including Mum's sister Clare or her parents, could have had the faintest idea of the type of people she had been mixing with for a long time. But that's hardly surprising – she didn't want anyone she knew to see her with them.

It was the beginning of winter and, because there was a staff training session, school came out early. As a result, we were home about an hour earlier than usual. Overhead, the sky was full of dark-grey clouds and we could feel dampness in the air. We had been offered a lift from one of Sid's friend's older brothers as rain was forecast and he didn't want his little brother getting soaking wet. We accepted gratefully as none of us had waterproof coats on and, as we set off, the first big drops of rain touched our cheeks. Relieved to be dry and home early, we were quite elated – that is until we walked into our home and met three people there who we would never have believed Mum would bring into the house.

Although we now had the truth just about thrown at us, we still did our best to remain with her. But what took place then comes a little later in my story ...

12

Mum must have heard us coming in as we always called out to her with a 'we're home, Mum', though this time there was no reply. She must have been a bundle of nerves when she heard us coming in – she certainly didn't get a chance to stop us walking into the living room, which I'm sure she wished she had been able to.

We must have looked pretty startled when we saw a group of people we had never seen before lounging about on our chairs and sofa. For a moment there was total silence as we couldn't think what to say. Nor could Mum, it seemed. When I caught Sid's eyes there was a blank look about them and I could tell that Mum was struggling to find words to explain who those people were. She didn't have any other choice than to introduce us to the two women, Karen and Julia, who were sat beside her on the sofa, first.

Their appearance caused all of us to stare a little. One had backcombed hair, dyed bright red, the other was blonde, though her roots were showing. They looked quite a lot older than Mum, but that hadn't stopped them from piling on more make-up than I had ever seen on a wrinkled face before. As for their trashy clothes – skintight short skirts and clinging, low-cut tops – I could hardly bring myself to look at them, I was so embarrassed.

The third person was a man of about 40 with a pronounced gut, a reddish face with slack, heavy jowls and beady, dark eyes that looked amused at our arrival. He didn't wait to be introduced but said with rather a smug smile, 'I'm Bill Slater, and you are …?' We gave him our names politely while he kept smiling. 'So, you three are Paula's children. What a nice-looking group you are! Get their good looks from you,' he said, turning towards Mum.

His clothes, unlike those of the two women, were I suppose quite smart and conventual. Which made me wonder why he was with those two, who hardly appeared thrilled at us being there. I could feel those eyes of his running up and down Lucy all the time we were in the room, which made me feel tense – there was something about him that made both Lucy and I feel quite nervous.

When the three of us were together after we left the room, we all said that we thought he was somewhat menacing. We just couldn't explain why, just that all three of us felt it.

Sid was remarkably brave that day as he refused to be intimidated by Bill. In fact, he tried his best to make him feel uncomfortable. I watched as he squared his shoulders and looked straight at him.

'You have a son at my school, haven't you?'

Lucy and I had a feeling that there was a reason for that

question. From the expression on the faces of the other two visitors, I guessed they must be thinking the same.

Before Bill could answer, Sid carried on speaking: 'It's just that I was sure I recognised you when I walked in. I tried to think where I had seen you before and then it came to me. I've seen you a few times outside the school gates – you were chatting to some of the senior boys. I didn't think much about it then, I just thought that you were the father of one of that group. Didn't you notice me?'

There was no answer, just a shrug and a smile with little warmth.

'You like your school then?'

I thought his question must be an attempt to change the subject. I saw that the two women were still not looking very happy and, when I glanced over at Mum, I noticed how her hands were clenched. That told me that she wished Sid would stop asking Bill questions. When I mentioned it to Lucy later that afternoon, she said that she had noticed that Mum was bothered, because Sid was known for always telling the truth – 'Mum knows he never lies.'

'I do like my school,' Sid replied after a couple of seconds' reflection. 'I'm lucky that I get on well with my teachers and the head, aren't I? But then I work hard. It's the head who often stops and has a chat with me about the exams I'll be taking in a couple of years. He wants to know about the career I would like to have.' He smiled at him then. 'Anyway, which of the boys is your son, or is he a nephew or a friend's boy, Bill?'

I saw the glare in Bill's eyes then as he replied, 'No, I think you've made a mistake – I don't go around any of the schools. Haven't got a son of that age. I don't even know what school you're in.'

Sid gave him the name.

'Oh, that one! No, I don't know anyone who goes there either.'

'Oh well, I must have got it wrong then,' Sid replied, his gaze fixed straight at Bill.

From the expressions on everyone's faces, I could tell that no one there thought for one moment that he didn't mean it.

Mum interjected, 'Enough questions now, Sid. Time for homework.' But she had left it a little late, for Sid had asked the ones that mattered.

'Oh, I don't mind,' said Bill blithely. 'I think your son's going to do very well at school.' Bill made his face crease into a smile as he spoke, but none of us thought it was sincere.

A few minutes later, when we were gathered together in the kitchen, we all agreed that there was something menacing about him.

It was wanting to get away from Bill and the other two that made us use the excuse that we had homework to do, which got us out of there. Lucy and I didn't have a desk in our room, which meant we usually worked on the dining-room table, so us going upstairs made Mum look even more embarrassed. Her face was flushed, but worse than that, which we all had noticed, her pupils had shrunk again. Sid already knew what had caused that and it didn't take long for Lucy and I to cotton on as well.

As Sid said, it was us coming in earlier than usual which

had caused our mother such discomfort. She must have been cringing inside when she realised that we had witnessed a part of her life that she had hoped to keep secret. We all decided that it was them who had left those empty bottles behind – 'Don't want to clear up their mess again when they leave,' Lucy announced furiously. 'No doubt she has them over when we're at school and gets them to leave before we come back.'

Sid still didn't tell us about the syringe he had found – he would only do so when he felt there was no alternative.

'I'm sure he's a drug dealer,' he said angrily, once we were upstairs. 'I don't want to ever see him here again, or those two witches he brought with him. Whatever does Mum think she's doing, mixing with people like that? I wasn't mistaken about seeing Bill talking to the older boys at my school either – I wish I'd looked a bit closer so I could find out the names of the ones he was talking to. There's a big drug problem, not just in my school, but in other ones as well, which is why the teachers have been talking to us about it.'

'This could ruin Mum's life as well,' Lucy said sadly. 'And what would Nan think? I just hope Mum's not taking them.'

But it wouldn't take long for Lucy and I to know that she did.

'Anyhow, now Bill knows I recognised him, he won't be hanging around my school any longer,' Sid concluded. 'He could tell that it wasn't just me boasting about getting on with the head, it was a warning.'

* * *

It was a few years later when we found out that Sid had been right. Even though I had taken a dislike to Bill, I still thought he was some kind of businessman who just gave drugs to people he knew. What I didn't have a clue about then was that the dealers at the top make a great deal of money. Large suitcases full of notes get hidden in various places and through various illegal means that money ends up in overseas banks. Bill eventually had a large business that employed a great many people working all over the UK. The worse part of that was that a lot of them were teenagers or even younger kids who were still at school. How do I know that? He and many of his dealers were finally arrested. The two women, who we had met more than once, were the ones who worked for him in the south of England. They took the large consignment of drugs that were smuggled in, wrapped them into small packets and handed them over to dealers, who in turn had a team working under them.

But that was all to come …

13

It was when we were all upstairs that the enormity of what we had just seen made us realise that Mum's life was falling apart. I felt tearful, Lucy looked shattered and even Sid seemed pale and reflective. Mum might have been embarrassed at us meeting that group of people, but embarrassed or not, would she stop mixing with them and letting them into our home? None of us wanted to see them in our home again, but would our mother put us first and get rid of them? That question was in all our heads.

About 20 minutes after going upstairs, we heard voices and laughter in the hall.

'They must be leaving,' Lucy said hopefully.

No sooner had she uttered those words than the women, making sure they were loud enough for us to hear, called up, 'Bye, you three.' We all thought that they didn't sound as though Mum had told them that they couldn't come back – their voices were far too cheerful for that.

Sid put his head around the door and waited until he heard

Mum say goodbye to Bill – he didn't want to bump into him if he was still there.

'Thank goodness that man has gone now,' he told us as he heard the front door shut. 'Look, I want to talk to Mum about today. You stay here until I come back up.'

We both nodded and Lucy said, 'All right, Sid, we'll stay here. I don't think Mum will be in the kitchen yet. I'm guessing she's lying on the sofa, wondering what to say to us.' But as Sid left the room, my sister said she wanted to hear what he asked her and what Mum said to him in return.

'I hope he doesn't close the downstairs door. We want to hear what's going on, don't we, Georgia?'

'Yes,' I agreed.

'Let's sit on the top step and do our best to listen. I think there's going to be trouble.'

She was right there, as it didn't take long for Mum to get angry.

Although Sid hadn't pulled the door shut, we could still only hear parts of the conversation until their voices began to rise.

'I know what those people were here for, Mum. I'm amazed that you let them into our house. As for that man, Bill, he's up to no good.'

We both heard that one sentence clearly, as we did some other parts of the conversation which I, in particular, found upsetting.

'You don't know Bill, so don't be so rude about him, Sid.'

'Come on, Mum! I wasn't making it up. I've seen him at my school gates and I know he's a dealer. And don't bother to tell me you're not taking drugs, I know you are. Don't you know how dangerous that is? That's why Dad got so angry with you.'

We heard her say that she didn't want to talk about Dad, and besides, she was not taking anything illegal either.

'Is that right, Mum? So, tell me why I found a syringe in the rubbish when you weren't well. That Bill's been round here more than a couple of times, hasn't he? We've had to throw out empty beer bottles and all the other mess they left when we cleaned up the kitchen. You don't drink beer, but he does – look, there's an empty bottle on the table.'

'God, you sound like your dad already, Sid.'

'That's because I don't believe you when you say you don't touch drugs, Mum. I don't want to see those people here again. If you're going to have them over, I'll go to Nan and Grandad's and stay there.'

'Look, Sid, they're my friends. I don't interfere with you and ask who you mix with after school. It's not as though you always come back here with your sisters, so what I do and who I spend time with is nothing to do with you. You're not a grown-up, so you don't know what you're saying. You're just a boy who's looked after and fed by me. So, mind your own business. It's my house, not yours, and Bill can come over any time he wants.'

'I believe he's one of the people who's been getting boys at my school to sell drugs for him. That's why I was telling him I'd seen him there, and I have, Mum, you must believe me.'

'Don't you dare insult my friends, you don't know anything.'

'Didn't you think that he lied about not knowing which

school we go to? I'm sure you told him a little about us. If I see him there again, I'm going straight to the head.'

Mum didn't say anything more, not then. There was silence for a few minutes, and I think they both felt more sad than angry. We then heard her voice, which sounded weary, finally say, 'Do what you want to do, Sid. I'm going to get us dinner now.'

When Sid came upstairs, I could tell how upset he was. Of course, he loved Mum, but after seeing those visitors, he really hated what was going on in his home. He was already convinced that Mum was on drugs and now he knew who was supplying them for her. Having those sorts of people around was simply too much for him. He told Lucy and I that he had made up his mind, he was going to talk to Nan the next day after school.

'About what?' Lucy asked innocently, even though after our eavesdropping we had a good idea what his reasons were.

'I'm going to ask Nan if we can all move in with her. She needs to know who's coming into our home,' he answered coolly.

'You should ask us what we want to do,' said Lucy a little crossly. 'I don't want to do any such thing. What about you, Georgia?'

'No, I want to stay with you and Mum, Lucy,' I told her.

'Good for you,' she said, patting me on the shoulder. She then turned to Sid: 'We don't want to leave Mum here on her own. What would Grandad think anyhow? He got this house for it to be a home for all of us, not just Mum, didn't he?'

'Yes, I get that, and why did he do it? It wasn't just for

Mum, it was because our grandparents want the best for us. They would have discussed it and then decided that growing up in a good home would be lot better for us than that awful place we were living in. But do you really think we're in a good home? Because I don't. Not with those kinds of visitors coming over anyway. And there are other things I don't like either. So, think about it, Lucy – you shouldn't be seeing things like we have and Georgia certainly shouldn't.'

When Sid went into his room, Lucy and I talked about it. We didn't want to think of Mum being lonely and on her own, and as Lucy said, who would look after her when she was unwell? It was that thought that made us decide to stay with her.

'We'll try to get Sid to give Mum another chance and not go to Nan's.'

But Sid was adamant: 'I've made up my mind, so don't keep trying to change it, Lucy. I'm still going to see Nan, and if she agrees, I'll be out of here in a couple of days. Wait and see, you'll be sorry about staying here. Then you'll be asking Nan if you can move in too.'

I suppose Lucy and I secretly hoped that Nan would refuse him. Maybe she would say, 'Grandad and I didn't get a house for you all only to have one of you leave it.'

But it only took a day for us to find out that she had said yes to him. I knew that he had gone to see her when I came out of my junior school and waited for Sid and Lucy to come. When I saw it was only my sister coming to walk home with me, I knew where Sid had gone. Mum didn't ask us where he was when we arrived home. She looked as though she had taken a bath, washed her hair and seemed, if not happy, then more together than she often was.

Lucy and I were doing our homework on the table when we heard the phone ring. We could tell it was Nan, even though we couldn't hear what she was saying. We could see that Mum was looking upset with what Nan must have been telling her about Sid's visit. All we heard her say was, 'If that's what he wants, then of course he can stay with you for a bit.'

It was quite a while before Sid came in. As neither of our grandparents came in with him, I guessed Grandad must have put him in a taxi. When Sid came in, he didn't sit down, but started to tell Mum where he'd been.

'I already know you've spent the afternoon with my parents,' she told him sharply.

Lucy and I glanced at each other, wondering if we could escape upstairs, as we heard Mum say coldly, 'I've had my mother on the phone, Sid. I'm sure you knew she was going to talk to me before you got back. Anyhow, I've agreed that you can stay in your grandparents' house for as long as you like. There's no point having you here, where you obviously don't want to be. But I'm curious what reason you gave them that you would rather be with them?'

'Just that I didn't like your friends that drop in and I want to be in a quieter place to do my homework.'

'Was that all you said?'

'Yes, Mum.'

She looked a little relieved at his reply, though Lucy and I could tell she was still upset. After all, she could have made a promise to Sid that she would make sure that our home life would be better and that she would no longer have those people in it.

I've known for a long time now why she couldn't. She might have denied her need for drugs when we were young, but by then she was already an addict. Just thinking of that, and how it ruined her life, still has the power to make me feel immensely sad.

Sid came into our room that evening.

'I'm going to move to Nan's tomorrow. You know why I'm leaving, don't you?' he said.

'Yes, you don't like Mum's friends.'

'There's more to it than that. It's not just about those people. I'm going to try and explain to you two again. You shouldn't stay here, there's something very wrong happening in this house. Those friends of hers are no good and they won't be going away.'

'What have you really told Nan?' my sister wanted to know.

'Just what I told Mum, Lucy. Nothing else. I didn't tell you both before, but remember when we saw the beer bottles? There was a syringe in the bin and that means really bad drugs, drugs that cause addiction and sometimes death. I kept quiet about it then and I didn't want to worry Nan too much, otherwise you two might not have a choice about staying here.'

'We can't leave Mum,' Lucy told him. 'She needs us to help her.'

We missed Sid terribly once he left, though we were able to see him at school. But Mum didn't see him again for a very long time.

14

It seemed to both Lucy and I that, almost every day since our brother had left, our lives there had got a whole lot worse. It was as if, without him there, Mum no longer cared much about our home or who came into it. We could tell by the empty beer bottles left in the kitchen that Bill had been visiting her more frequently, but at least he was gone before we got back from school.

Over the coming weeks, the house began to look more and more neglected. As for meals, most of the time it was Lucy who had to cook them. Mum seemed to have gone back to lying around and giving us excuses such as she had a headache. Every so often, when we came back from school and walked in, our hearts would lift when we saw she was up and about. The house and kitchen would be clean and a vacuum cleaner had finally left the cupboard, without Lucy having to lift it out. Those days she made a tasty meal for us and then we would sit together at dinner time, chatting happily together. On the bad days, the vacuum stayed in its cupboard, while the dusters and small brushes kept it company.

On weekends, it was usually Lucy who was in charge of the washing machine. Between us, we managed to do all our bedding and laundry and keep on top of it, as well as our schoolwork. We were still so young so were determined to stay with her.

It seemed that, a lot of the time, Lucy had to assume the role of my mother, instead of just being my older sister. On the days when Mum had gone back to feeling so tired that not one cup had been washed up all day, Lucy told me she felt sorry for her. She would do her best to look after Mum, as well as having to get a meal for us all. It was a good thing that Lucy had learnt to cook from an early age or I don't know how we would have managed. Takeaway pizzas and eggs, I suppose.

Those days, when Mum was either on the sofa or had gone back to bed, we also had the house to try to keep clean and our homework suffered. That was how we filled our spare time. If Mum was lying around with the television on and nothing to say to us, at least without Sid not being there, we were able to do our homework at the desk in his room. When his stuff went to Nan's, his desk and bookcase remained behind – he had told us that we might need it and he was right.

It might sound as though our lives were not that good, but those days were only the beginning of what was to become much worse. The day everything turned into a nightmare for us was the one when we had been invited to tea at Nan's. That invitation had been extended because it was my ninth birthday. My grandparents wanted me to have a special one and let's just say it ended up being far from that.

They had not only invited Mum, Lucy and me, but some of our other relatives on Mum's side were also expected to join in the celebration. Mum's beautiful younger sister Clare, who I really loved, would be there. She was the one person I was really excited about seeing.

'We'd better be extra clean and tidy if we're going to Nan's,' Lucy said with a grin. 'You know, faces and hands scrubbed clean and let's choose our clothes and I'll give them a quick iron.'

By then Mum never ironed our clothes and we mostly relied on the wind to blow out the creases on the washing line. Lucy and I would always look at the weather to decide if we were wearing our school jumpers. If so, only the collars and cuffs on our school shirts would be ironed.

'I'll do them this evening and put them out on Sid's bed so we can change quickly when we get back,' my sister offered. 'I'm sure Mum will look great as well.'

'I expect she will,' I said cautiously.

After all, I knew that Mum would not let her mother see her looking anything other than her best.

Lucy pulled me upstairs so that we could sort out what we wanted to wear the next evening. She rummaged through our wardrobes and picked out a dress for me, a dark-blue one – 'Nan gave you that, so it's a good one to wear,' she told me as she laid it out on the bed and pulled another one out for herself. 'They could do with a quick press,' she added, taking them downstairs.

* * *

The next morning, Mum had looked fresh and happy when we came down for breakfast. As soon as I walked into the living room, she gave me a hug. 'Happy birthday, darling,' she said as she hugged me gently and kissed the top of my head.

It was the first time in several days that she had got up before us. We woke up when she called through our door to let us know that she was going down to make our breakfast. For the first time in weeks, I could smell bacon frying. She had already laid the table and there was a little parcel and an envelope propped up at my place.

'You can open it now, darling,' she told me as she sat down.

Which was enough to make my small fingers undo the paper fairly quickly. I had guessed by its shape what was in it and I was right: it was the Swatch wristwatch that I had been wanting for a while. That put a smile on my face.

'I love it, Mum! Promise I'll take good care of it,' I said as I slid off my chair and kissed her on the cheek.

For once I was looking forward to coming back home after school. Going over to Nan's would be great and I could hardly wait to see everyone. I knew I would be made a fuss of, with lots of hugs and kisses, not to mention presents. Like other birthdays, Nan would have made a special cake with candles on it. I would have to blow them out and make a wish before I could open my parcels and cards.

Within seconds of my sister and I walking through the school gates, a lot of the other juniors came rushing over to wish me a happy birthday. Lucy gave me a hug. 'See you on our break,' she said, before making her way to the senior's.

It was hard for me to concentrate in class that day, especially as there were loads of cards given to me by my classmates. If they made me happy, the one the teacher handed over to me made me even more so. 'Your dad sent it here for you,' she told me.

For months I had been wondering where he was and why we never saw him. Ever since Mum had made us flee from our home after their last row, I missed him so much. More than once I had asked her where he was, but all she told me was that he wasn't in the area anymore.

I think my hands were shaking when I opened the envelope and took out the enormous, beautiful card. It had a picture of a little girl on it with a pink birthday cake laid out on a tiny table next to her. Inside there were 'happy birthday' wishes and underneath, he had written saying that he was going to take me out on the next Saturday – 'I 'have something special planned for you then, darling.'

I was very excited that I was finally going to see my dad again in just a couple of days. As I wriggled on my classroom chair with joy, I couldn't wait to tell Lucy and Sid. I guessed that Mum would be none too pleased to have him come to the house to pick me up, but I also knew he wouldn't have written that to me if he hadn't already talked to her on the phone. She must have agreed that he could see us and that I could have a day out with him.

I wished he could also have been at Nan's that evening so that he could wish me a happy birthday on the actual day. At that time, I wasn't fully aware of what he had done to make my grandparents so angry or why they wouldn't want him in their house.

I looked out of the window and imagined what the rest of the day was going to be like. It might not be a party like a few of the ones I had been to when one of my school friends had a birthday. Depending on the weather, these often took place in the living room of their homes or out in the garden, which was better. My party was going to be very different because there would be no other children apart from my sister and brother, but I was still really looking forward to it. I loved being with my grandparents and the relatives, and it meant more time with Sid as well.

Sid met me in the playground when we were all having our first break of the day. I got a bear hug from him as he wished me a happy birthday. He lifted me off the ground and spun around with me.

'It'll be a good evening for you, Georgia,' he told me. 'Nan's been pretty busy making sure you'll have a special time. I'll see you later and I've got a present for you too.'

'What is it, Sid?'

'You'll have to wait till you come over, won't you, baby Sis?' he said, while poking me in the ribs, which made me giggle.

I told him excitedly about the card from Dad and that he was going to take me out the next weekend.

'I hope he gives you a great day out,' he said, though I noticed that he made no further comment on this.

The rest of my day at school seemed to go very slowly. As soon as the bell rang for the end of the day, I trotted out to more calls of 'happy birthday!', clutching my pile of cards, to wait at the gate for Lucy. We were both in a happy mood when we began walking home. She, too, was looking forward to seeing all the family: 'I love Nan's cooking, especially her birthday teas, and I expect she's done something really special for you. Now when we get home, let's go straight upstairs and put on our dresses!'

'And scrub my hands and face,' I said, grinning.

Lucy laughed at that before adding, 'I bet Mum will be already dolled up and looking great when we get there.'

'She'll have had all day to get ready,' I noted as I forced my legs to keep up with my older sibling's longer strides.

As soon as we reached the door to our house and opened it, we called out, 'Mum, we're back!' as usual.

Silence.

'Don't tell me she's still getting ready,' Lucy sighed as we stood at the bottom of the stairs and called out again.

'Are you up there, getting your face on?' she yelled. 'We're here!'

More silence.

'She must be in the kitchen. Better find her,' Lucy said as we walked towards the living room, which led to it.

I was just behind Lucy when she pushed open the door and she cried out the word 'Mum!' before rushing in. When I saw the reason for her concern, I began to shake. Mum lay motionless on the floor. That frightened me and I felt a lump come into my throat. Lucy was already on her knees beside her when I, too, got down on the floor.

'Mum, what's happened to you?' Lucy kept saying, but Mum didn't move.

I thought she must be dead and so I screamed before bursting into tears.

At the time, Lucy was far too upset about Mum to try to calm me down. 'Mum, come on, open your eyes,' she kept saying again and again. It was then that she noticed the cord round Mum's upper arm and the syringe that was only a few inches from her hand – she must have dropped it when she fell. There were also drops of blood near it.

Lucy tried hard not to cry – she was still only eleven but knew a lot more about drugs than I did. I didn't understand what Mum had done to cause her to pass out, but Lucy did.

'Is she dead, Lucy?' I asked through my sobs.

'She's not dead, Georgia,' she told me. 'She's still breathing. So stop crying, take a deep breath and go and wash your face. I've got to ring Nan, she'll know what to do.'

Pulling herself up straight, Lucy went to the phone. She was trembling so much that she found it difficult to get the number right. I could tell then that she was just as frightened as me. When she heard Nan's voice answering the phone, she stuttered with fear and could barely get her words out. The ones I understood were 'on the floor', 'syringe' and 'not moving'.

Mum's secret was well and truly out. Lucy had no other choice than to tell Nan exactly what she knew, though I noticed she still kept quiet about the visitors who came to the house. No doubt Sid, who would be furious as well as concerned when he heard about Mum, would feel obliged to tell her everything else.

Nan must have said something that calmed Lucy sufficiently for her to be able to answer some questions. My sister's voice changed slightly and I heard her say, 'Yes, there's a tight-looking rubber band on her arm just above her elbow.'

Nan must have needed as many details as possible so she could call 999 and explain why an ambulance was needed at our house. Just the fact that there were only two young girls there with their unconscious mother would have encouraged them to come as fast as they could.

I heard Lucy say, 'How long will it take?' and then, 'OK, Nan,' before she put the phone down.

'Nan and Aunt Clare are coming over as soon as she's rung for an ambulance,' she told me. 'The hospital's not far from here, so it won't be long. Nan's not far from us either, so maybe they'll all get here together at the same time.'

What she didn't tell me was that Nan had asked if Mum's breathing was shallow and she had answered, 'I think so, but she's face down.'

I hadn't realised at the time what that meant.

Trying my best not to cry again, I kept looking at Mum lying on the floor. Lucy was already kneeling down beside her again and pushed her hand under Mum as far as her fingers could go. She was trying to feel for a heartbeat in Mum's chest and she looked worried.

'Think you'd better sit by the window and take some deep breaths. Then you can watch out for the ambulance,' she told me. 'She's breathing, Georgia. The doctor will make her better.'

Lucy came and sat down beside me, and placed her arm around my shoulders. Those words of comfort still couldn't stop the tears from flowing down my cheeks. It might have been minutes, but it seemed like hours to me before we heard the siren and then spotted the ambulance coming up our road.

Lucy and I saw the flashing light as the ambulance pulled up and two paramedics carrying small cases climbed out. In her shocked state, Lucy rushed to the door, saying, 'They're here now, Mum,' even though our mother was unable to reply.

I could hear her saying, 'She's in there,' so she must have pointed her finger towards the living room. In a matter of seconds the paramedics walked in. One of them, a woman, told us both gently to stay sitting on the sofa while they took care of Mum: 'We're going to turn her over now,' she said as they both knelt down on either side of her.

I watched as they gently turned my mother so that she was lying on her side. One of them took off the rubber strap that was on Mum's arm. It was seeing how pale she was and that her eyes were still closed that caused more tears to stream down my cheeks; I gripped Lucy's hand really tightly. Over the next few minutes our eyes were glued to those two paramedics as we watched every movement they made. I saw the woman feel for a pulse in Mum's throat while the man placed a stethoscope on her chest over where her heart was. He whispered to his colleague, who had moved her fingers to Mum's wrist. It was later on, when Lucy got me to put my hand on her wrist so she could explain what a pulse was.

I remember feeling sick when that syringe was picked up and looked at. More whispering came then before a gloved hand dropped it into a plastic bag. It was put into one of the cases they had brought with them. It was then that I saw a small mask being put over Mum's nose as well as her mouth. Lucy put her arm around me when she heard me trying to ask, 'What's that for?' and drew my head onto her shoulder.

Aware that we were watching them, the woman medic smiled in our direction: 'It's only to help her breathing,' she told us.

'You see, Georgia, they're going to get Mum better,' Lucy whispered in my ear. However brave my sister might have been, I could sense she was fighting to keep her own tears back – she was still only 11, after all.

A few minutes later, to our huge relief, we heard the front door opening again and the hurried footsteps of Nan and Aunt Clare as they came in. Nan shot us a grim smile and said something about how maybe we would be better going upstairs with Clare. Then by the way Lucy looked at her, she realised that we didn't want to leave Mum. 'All right, just stay where you are,' she said as she moved over to talk to the paramedics.

Clare knelt down a little so we could see each other's faces clearly before she spoke. 'Your mum's going to be all right,' she told us. 'Let's go into the kitchen while Nan talks to the paramedics and get out some glasses. I've brought some juice with me – I'm sure you must be thirsty now.' I hadn't realised that I was until she spoke. 'OK,' was my reply and I went to the kitchen with my aunt and Lucy.

However calm Clare might have been trying to be, Lucy could tell she looked shocked at what she saw when she came in. She quickly put a smile on her face for us to see, but that must have been hard for her – she would have known far more than us about the harm that overdosing on heroin can do, for that was what it was. Seeing her older sister on the floor like that must have been just about as frightening for her as for us.

I'm sure those medics would have been relieved when both Nan and Clare arrived. At last, they had people there who would look after two distressed children – ones they didn't want to tell just how serious their mum's collapse had been. The female medic looked up at us quickly when we came out of the kitchen: 'We're going to take your mum to hospital now. Don't worry, she'll be well looked after.'

More tears sprang to my eyes. 'Is Mum going to die?' I finally managed to ask.

'Of course she isn't, my darling.' Nan came and hugged us to her. 'Now, Georgia, no more tears. You've just heard that she'll be well looked after so stop worrying so much, everything's going to be all right. Now, I'm going in the ambulance and Clare will look after you two.'

Nan was right to take a pragmatic stance for I stopped crying immediately. Even now I can still admire how she managed not to show how she really felt that day. Turning to Clare first, she said, 'You can help them pack a few things, so they can stay with us for a little while,' before adding, 'Now, girls, Clare will take you over to my house as soon as she's sorted out everything that you'll need. Don't forget your school things. I'm going to go now, the ambulance is going to the hospital. As soon as I get back, I'll be able to tell you how your mother is.'

She didn't say that Grandad stayed at home so that he could phone everyone who had been invited over and explain why it would be better if they didn't come. He also had to let Sid know what had happened. That would not have been easy for him. He was aware of why Sid had left home, even though they had not been told everything, but that didn't mean that his grandson didn't still love his mother. All Sid had wanted was for her to stop taking drugs and mixing with those people, who were the ones who had supplied her.

Grandad's plan was that, as soon as Clare was back in the house with us, he could leave and go to the hospital. He knew that, although Nan was able to hide her emotions in front of us, she would need him there. Watching their daughter fighting for her life is one of the worst things in any parent's life. How my nan and Clare managed to be with us without either of them shedding a tear was beyond me – it must have been more than difficult.

I can remember one of the medics telling Lucy and I that Mum's eyes were fluttering a little, which was a good sign. Of course, that was said to help us feel a little better, though I think Nan and Clare must have understood what might still happen in the hospital. But still they managed not to show their feelings, even when Mum was rolled onto a stretcher. It was lifted onto a trolley and wheeled out of the door. By now the neighbours had gathered, as they always do when an ambulance arrives. Lucy and I followed them out and watched as the stretcher holding our mother went into the ambulance.

'I'll see you two soon,' Nan told us, as she climbed into the back of the ambulance with the female medic. The other one shut the door swiftly, then climbed into the driver's seat. The flashing blue light came on and we could hear the siren blaring as they drove off at a fast pace.

Clare put her arms round us and said, 'She's going to get

better, so no more crying. Let's go up to your room and sort out what you need.'

'How long do you think we'll be at Nan's?' Lucy asked anxiously.

'Not long, I'm sure,' Clare said as she ushered us back in the house. 'Just a few days, till your mum's better. Now, when we get to Nan's house, Grandad wants to drive over to the hospital and bring Nan back but they might not come straight back. He'll also want to spend a little time with your mum. So, let's get ready now so that he can go.'

It was not until we got upstairs and saw Lucy's and my dresses on Sid's bed that the memory of what the day was meant to be all about came flooding back to me. I turned to Clare and asked, 'Is it still my birthday party?'

'Oh, darling,' she said as she hugged me, 'I know this has been a terrible day for you. Now listen, it's just going to be us at Nan's house tonight – we didn't think you'd want to be with more than just us this evening. Nan and I will arrange another birthday party for you once your mother's home. How does that sound?'

'Better,' I said, forcing a smile. 'I don't want to open any of my presents until Mum comes home.'

'Good for you! I'm sure you and Lucy are feeling quite tired already, but maybe we can have some cake when we get there – it's all out on the table anyway.'

Lucy agreed that taking our dresses now was pointless so we tried to think what we might need and put a few changes of clothes together as well as our school things.

Clare must have been pleased that I had agreed with

her about my birthday being postponed. Another thing she didn't tell us was that having a houseful of relatives over would have been too much for our grandparents. With her daughter in hospital, Nan was much more stressed than she would let us see.

Clare went into Mum's room and found a large zip-up bag to put some of our clothes in. When that was packed, we went into the bathroom and picked up our toiletries.

'Now, let's get over to Grandad,' said Clare. 'He'll be waiting for us and so will Sid. He knows about Nan going to the hospital with Mum.'

Although Lucy had keys to the house, Clare asked for them and told us to get in the car while she checked that all the windows were shut and that the place was safely locked up. Soon afterwards we set off for our grandparents' house.

I can't remember much about the rest of that day, apart from being with Sid. He was waiting for us in the hall and I do remember him looking almost as pale as Mum had been. It was Clare he directed a couple of questions to.

'Is it because I left that everything has got worse?' he asked.

'No, Sid, nothing would have changed, even if you had stayed,' Clare said kindly. 'Your mum needs help to put a stop to what she's doing. Nan will do her best to help sort that out, but first, she has to get better and in that hospital she will.'

'I hope so, I want my old Mum back, so do the girls,' he said sadly.

And that's all I can remember of that day. Was there cake? I suppose there must have been.

Nan and Grandad were still not back when we went to bed.

15

Neither Lucy nor I went to school for the next few days. Nan had phoned the Head to explain that our mother had been rushed to hospital and was in intensive care. Being on our own when we found her, we had also witnessed the paramedics working on her unconscious body and it had caused both of us to be in shock, anxious and very tearful. Nan thought we were too distressed to go to school and it would be better if we had a couple of days' rest before we returned to our classes. Not that any mention was made of the cause of Mum's collapse.

The Head evidently was wholeheartedly sympathetic about what we had gone through and said that, of course, she understood. She also told Nan that we were both bright pupils and we would have no difficulty in catching up on a couple of days' classes. That must have pleased Nan no end and, when she told Lucy and I about the conversation over our breakfast, she was beaming with pride.

Clare had come into our bedroom earlier that morning. 'Hope you two slept well,' she said. We had, and somewhat surprisingly, had both fallen asleep almost straight away after we tumbled into our beds. The warm milk that Clare had given us must have helped, we told her.

'Good, you needed that,' she said. 'I just came to tell you that I'm going to the hospital this morning.'

'Can we come with you?' we asked in unison.

'It's not a visiting time,' she said firmly. 'The ward Sister's allowing me to go in for just for a few minutes because I want to find out how she's getting on and what she might need Nan to bring in this afternoon. The Sister did tell me a bit of good news, though: your mum's recovering quite well, but for now, she can only have one visitor at a time in the ward she's in. As soon as I get back here and you've made me one of your cups of tea, Lucy, we can all sit down together and I'll tell you how she is and how long she's likely to be in there – I don't think it's going to be very long. Now, any messages for her?'

We were both feeling nervous after Clare left, but in her bag she had little messages quickly scribbled by each of us. Once we had managed to eat our breakfast, Nan suggested we go into the living room, put the TV on and wait for Clare to return. Eager to please, we agreed to this. Now all Lucy and I could do was to hope that our mum was getting better and that she would be home soon.

It must have been about half an hour later when Nan brought through a tray of tea and biscuits for us. 'Help yourselves, girls,' she told us before she went back in the kitchen to do some more cooking. I'm convinced that she must have wanted to busy herself because she, too, was waiting to hear what Clare had to say when she returned. As Nan was trying to keep our minds off Mum being in hospital, she didn't say anything about Clare being there when she came in and out of the room.

It seemed a very long time before our ears pricked up at the sound of Clare's car coming to a halt outside the house. In fact, when I looked down at my shiny new watch, I saw it was only about 90 minutes since she had left. Lucy and I just about had our fingers crossed as we so badly wanted to hear some positive news; we felt even more optimistic when we saw the wide smile on Clare's face.

She sat down close to us and said, 'Before you ask, I can tell you that your mum's looking a lot better and she loved your little notes to her.' From the relaxed way that Clare had come in, we felt immediately relieved – she seemed a lot less worried about her sister than before she left.

'She was still a little sleepy when I got there,' Clare continued. 'But she managed to sit up a bit and talk, which told me it won't be long before she comes home. They hope to move her out of intensive care this lunchtime and onto a normal ward.'

Hearing those words made us ask again when we could go to the hospital and see her.

'You'll be able to go in a couple of days when she has a little more energy. The ward nurse told me that it's important that she doesn't get too tired, so it's one visitor a day at the moment. Your mum asked me lots of questions about you two – I think she was worried about you finding her like that. I made sure that she didn't think you were cross with her. I told her that all you wanted was for her to come home.'

Hearing what Mum had said about what had happened brought tears to our eyes as well.

'Now, don't cry,' Clare told us. 'I've already had to stop your mother doing that! Of course, she was upset about what you had gone through. I told her it was you, Lucy, who managed to make the phone call which saved her and that you're both being well looked after here. Let's get some more tea – I need it.'

The three of us went into the kitchen where Nan was. She also appeared relieved – Clare had quickly given her the news before she came to talk to us. A smile was on her face when she asked, 'Are you looking for tea, Clare?' Without waiting for an answer, she switched on the kettle.

The day seemed to pass slowly and we were wondering how Sid must be feeling. When he came in from school, he went straight to Clare and Nan to ask how our mother was. He might not have changed his mind about living with her, but I could tell he was more than relieved that she was beginning to recover.

Although Sid wanted to know if she was getting better, I noticed that he didn't ask if he could visit her in hospital. He clearly still wanted to keep a distance between them. Mum hadn't mentioned him either, Clare admitted, when I raised it after my brother had gone upstairs to do his homework.

'I know your mum feels sad about never seeing him, but she understands why that is,' she told me. 'But I can see that he still cares about her.'

At dinner it was much more relaxed than the previous night – we all felt so much better now that we knew Mum was recovering. In a few days Lucy and I could visit her in hospital – a visit that never happened.

On the day that we were due to visit Mum, just as we were leaving for school, the phone rang. It was the Ward Sister, who told Nan that her daughter had been seen by a doctor and that she was well enough to go home.

'I had asked your mum when I visited last night if she would like to stay here with us for a few days when she left the hospital – I thought it would be better for her if she could just rest for a while. But she said she wants to go back to her own home. Even so, when I collect her this morning, I'll ask again but I doubt she'll agree,' Nan told us.

There was a pause.

'Now, what do you two want to do?' she asked my sister and I.

'Go back to the house and help look after her a bit,' Lucy said quickly.

'I want to be with her too,' I told Nan, which made her smile.

'I thought so,' was all she said in return, before adding, 'Clare and I are going to drop you at school so you're not late, then get some groceries for you all before we drive over to the hospital and pick her up. We'll stay there with her till you arrive back from school.'

Even though my nan had smiled and sounded cheerful, I don't believe for one moment that was what she wanted us to say.

'You can always come and talk to me if there are any more problems. Just promise me you will.'

'I promise I'll ring you, Nan,' Lucy said, without saying what would make her pick up the phone and call for help again.

As we would still be in lessons when Mum arrived back, we were more than a little disappointed that we couldn't be in the house the moment she arrived home – we so wanted to be there to welcome her.

That all happened over 25 years ago, but even now I can still remember the happiness I felt when I walked into the house and saw Mum standing there. I felt her arms wrapping around me as she whispered that she was so pleased that Lucy and I were home and that we were all together again. I can remember that day as clearly as I can another one, which was to occur just a couple of months later.

16

We had desperately wanted to get back home as quickly as we could. Once school was over for the day, Lucy came straight to where I was waiting at the school gates. Both of us usually liked to see Sid, but this time we didn't wait for him, we just rushed out of the gates without giving him a thought and walked home as fast as we could.

Both Clare and Nan were still with Mum as they had promised. There were lots of hugs and I felt quite tearful because I was so pleased that Mum was there. She looked better than I had thought she might – pink cheeks, shiny hair and a wide smile that made us feel that we had the mother we loved so much back again.

Nan and Clare left soon after we arrived. Clare had brought over our bag with all our bits and pieces that had been at Nan's. Once it was only us three in the house, Mum told us to sit back down because she had something important she wanted to say. Lucy and I perched on the edges of our chairs as we waited to hear what it was that she wanted to tell us. First, she thanked us for being so brave when she had to be taken to the hospital. Then she apologised profusely for the shock we must have had when we walked in and found her. She told us that she had come to understand the harm her taking drugs had caused. Not just putting her in hospital, but upsetting both her parents and her children.

'I can't tell you how sorry I am,' she said, looking flushed. 'I know that I've made your life difficult and I'm so grateful that the pair of you have decided to stay with me. I could only blame myself if you had told your nan and grandad that you no longer wished to live with me. And I'll tell you this, when I woke up in hospital and realised why I was in there, I had time to think about the ways I have failed you. To think, it was you two who saved my life. If you hadn't made that phone call, Lucy, I wouldn't be here now.'

Now that shocked us.

I could see then that Mum looked really upset, her eyes were filling with tears: 'It was knowing what you had gone through and how you saved me that has made me determined to change my life. Not for my own sake, but for both of you and the rest of our family as well.'

More hugs came then, as did the tears from all three of us.

At my tender age, I truly believed all the promises that my mother made that day: no drugs in the house, no visits from Bill and his women, our breakfast would be made every day, the house would be kept clean and tidy, and even better, she would spend more time with us, especially at weekends. Those promises were enough to convince my sister and I that our lives would be like they used to be.

'I hope she doesn't find it hard managing on her own,' Lucy said.

That remark came after listening to why Mum was a little annoyed with both her sister and Nan. It was after she had explained to us how the plan she had in her head would change her life. Nan, on the other hand, had her own idea, which she had explained to Mum when they returned from the hospital.

'I just can't agree with what she wants me to do,' Mum told us and, from the tone of her voice, we could tell that she had resented whatever her mother's advice had been. When we heard a bit more about Nan's wishes, we were both on Mum's side, perhaps because we didn't really understand Nan's reasoning.

'What was it that Nan wanted you to do then?' Lucy asked.

'She wants to take me to a place miles away from here, so that I can spend weeks with other addicts.' Mum told us. 'Look, here's a leaflet about the place that your nan left for me to read.'

It was only then that I learnt that my mother might be an addict.

'It's a huge house, isn't it?' I said, trying my hardest to sound cheerful, as I glanced at the photo of an imposing red-brick house, stood in a well-maintained garden with beds of brightly coloured flowers and a large outside table with several chairs placed around it.

'Yes, it's pretty large, and no doubt bursting with sad people,' Mum replied. 'Goodness knows how many are staying there. It's a place where different types of addicts, whose families have decided they need help to stop drinking or taking drugs, are taken. They believe that, after a couple of months, the treatment they are given will stop them ever wanting to take drugs or drink alcohol again. Well, that's the message the people in charge give out and the patients' families must just hope it works. But I'm not like those people, I'm not an addict – I can stop any time.'

I was still looking down at the picture of the house while Mum was talking – both the house and the gardens looked beautiful to me. Still, I didn't know what it might be like inside. Studying the leaflet did change my mind a little, as it did Lucy's. Going there might do Mum good was one thought running through my head.

'It looks like an expensive hotel, Mum,' said Lucy when she, too, looked at the leaflet.

'Yes, I know what its appearance tells you. Like it's a great place to spend a weekend in. But it's not a hotel like your dad and I used to go to, with room service or fancy menus in the restaurants. Nor is there a wine list and certainly no bar to have a drink with a friend. Don't let the photos fool you. It's a rehab place, which costs even more than a smart hotel would. To be fair, your nan and grandad would pay for it but I'm not interested – I don't think I need it.'

I wanted to ask what happens there to make people like her better, but hardly taking a breath, Mum continued to tell us more about that place, looking at us to make sure we were listening properly.

'I understand why some people who have similar problems to me decide to go there. They don't believe that they will ever be able to give up either the drugs or alcohol damaging them and people around them without a lot of help. But I'm not like that – I'm convinced that I can manage on my own.'

'What treatment do they give?' Lucy asked.

'Goodness knows! Apart from us telling a roomful of people about being ashamed of what we've been taking, I haven't a clue. Whatever they are, I'm sure I would hate them. Anyhow, I've told your nan that I've already spoken to one of the doctors in the hospital and he gave me a lot of information to help me.'

That was more or less the end of our conversation, except that Mum then added, 'Thank goodness you two came in then – that stopped them going on about it!'

We had swallowed just about everything Mum told us, though that didn't stop us wondering if rehab might be easier for her. Still, she seemed very definite in what she said, which made us feel that she meant every word.

Sadly, it took just a few weeks before the need for drugs took over. She did try, I give her that – she wanted to keep to her promise to us, but she just couldn't. Not only did the drugs creep back into our house, so, too, did the group of people we couldn't stand.

17

The Sunday after Mum came home was the one that I was going to be taken out by Dad for my birthday treat. Mum told me he had arranged with her to pick me up from the house. I could tell she wasn't happy about it.

She said that I was free to see him if I wanted to. Which, of course, I did, but she did everything to make me feel guilty about my decision.

'He's your father and I can tell you're pleased that he's coming over to take you out. That's all right with me, I don't mind if all of you want to spend time with him. But I don't want to see him. It would be better for me if you wait outside for him.'

'All right, Mum, I will,' I told her.

When Sunday morning came, I couldn't help smiling at the thought of spending nearly a whole day with Dad. But then I was still young enough to have forgotten how certain aspects of his past behaviour had upset me.

Lucy didn't seem in the least bit bothered that she had not

been invited too: 'It's because he missed your birthday that he wants to take you out. You can tell me everything about your time with him when you get back. Besides, I'd better keep Mum company.'

That first time when Dad came for me, he arrived bang on time in a shiny black car that I had never seen before. No sooner had it pulled up outside than he flung open his door and jumped out.

'Oh, Georgia! I'm so happy to see you at last,' he said as he hugged me so hard that my feet left the ground. 'You've grown taller,' he added as he put me back down.

I could hardly stop myself from giggling with pleasure. Being tall with dark hair and blue eyes framed by thick lashes, he looked so handsome that day. I felt proud to call him my dad and to be going out with him. I admired how he was dressed too, in his smart casual clothes, especially that dark-blue jacket, which had always suited him. I wished I could bump into some of my school friends so that they would see my dad was the most handsome and best-dressed one ever.

'In you get, Princess,' he told me as he opened the car door for me.

'Where are we going, Dad?' I asked once he had made sure that my seat belt was on properly.

'Southend,' he told me. 'There's a funfair there, lots of things like rides, which I think you will love. I thought I'd take you for a walk on the beach first, though, so you can stretch your legs before we go onto the rides.'

As he drove, the pair of us chatted away. I can't remember what we talked about, just that it was relaxed and I enjoyed talking to him. We did as he suggested, a walk on the beach, had an ice cream and then, as we reached the funfair, my eyes opened wide – there really was a lot to do. My first choice was to go on the bumper cars and that was really fun. My second was going up in the sky on the Ferris wheel. I found that amazing and I could see loads of things once we reached the highest spot!

Dad then took me to a cafe for lunch and I chose fish and chips followed by a dessert of meringues and ice cream. It was there that he said, 'I think it's time to give you your birthday present.' A small package was pushed in front of me. My fingers fumbled with excitement as I opened it to find a silver charm bracelet, which had me beaming with pleasure. I jumped up and gave him a hug as a way of saying thank you and then I put it on straight away.

That was my first Sunday out with him. He told me he had really enjoyed the day and, when we drove into our road, he said he would be back on a Sunday soon and Lucy and Sid could join us as well, if they would like to. I was happy that Mum had said he had a right to spend time with us.

Lucy said yes, but she had already made arrangements with friends over the next couple of Sundays, while Sid answered a very firm no – 'You two go and have fun, but I don't want to see him. What he did was wrong.'

Dad didn't make any comment or even ask me why Sid had not appeared once when we went out for the third Sunday outing, this time with Lucy joining us. He seemed really pleased to see her and told us that we were going to Southend again. For the first part of the day, we really enjoyed ourselves – that is until we stopped for lunch.

It was the questions Dad asked that spoilt the day. I could tell that Lucy really objected to them. It was when we had gone to the stall to get hot dogs that the atmosphere between us began to change. No sooner were we sitting down on the benches than he blurted out that he knew Mum had been in hospital – 'So, girls, what caused her to be taken there?'

My guess now is that he had a pretty good idea.

Lucy, who remembered more about Dad than I did, certainly wasn't surprised at him bringing up that subject. As she had no intention of letting him know the facts, she managed to look fairly blank.

'I don't know what it was really,' she said calmly. 'She was only in for a short while, so it wasn't anything serious, thank goodness.'

'You're a bright girl, Lucy. Didn't you notice before the ambulance was called that she was unwell?'

'No, but then we leave for school early, and when we come back, we're busy with our homework. We have our dinner together, of course, but she didn't mention anything.'

'And how about now? Any signs that she's not totally recovered?' he persisted and I saw the piercing look in his eyes as he put that question to her.

'I'm sure she's just fine,' Lucy told him firmly. 'She looks really healthy and happy.'

Which up until then was the truth. If only that had lasted longer was what we both felt less than a week later.

Lucy and I didn't know then what Dad's reasons for trying to find out more information about Mum were. We were both shocked and frightened when we found out.

18

There are days of my childhood that I've done my best to erase from my memory. However hard I've tried, there are some that remain firmly planted in my mind. The following episode is one that I have never been able to forget.

The day that the need for the drugs finally overcame Mum was a Tuesday. I can remember that because it was only two days after Dad had asked Lucy those questions. Lucy had been so loyal to our mother when she refused to let on why Mum had been taken into hospital. That's what love can do, especially a child's love for a parent. It brings out 100 per cent loyalty. Neither of us had forgotten the promise Mum had made and we never dreamt that she would fail us.

Our faith in her disappeared that Tuesday when we walked into our home after school. One glance at the sofa where our dazed-looking mother lay told us that the demons had returned to haunt her.

I'm sure that Lucy must have felt as sick as I did as we took in the reality of what we were confronted with.

'Shall I make you a cup to tea, Mum?' she immediately asked. Her mind must have flown back to the past, when we had to face this so often when we returned from school.

I stood there feeling so disappointed and upset that I was unable to talk. Mum could hardly lift her head up when Lucy asked her about tea. She managed to mumble, 'Yes please, Lucy,' in the slurred voice I had hoped never to hear again.

Lucy and I looked at each other. Our expressions were telling each other that our biggest mistake was in believing that her drug problem was over. I felt so let down, I just wanted to cry. I had trusted Mum's promise, a promise that had made me feel both secure and happy again. I could hardly bear the thought of our lives going back to how they had been before she ended up in hospital. Neither of us would want to hear any more of those old excuses, such as she had caught a cold or had a headache and was tired.

At least following Lucy into the kitchen stopped me looking at Mum, who seemed oblivious to my presence and still hadn't spoken a word to me. Needless to say, there was a pile of crockery that needed washing as well as several glasses. Lucy put the kettle on as soon as we went in. 'Better make her that tea,' was just about all she said but for once she ignored the dirty dishes and all the used glasses. While we waited for the kettle to whistle, we looked around and found what we expected: empty wine and beer bottles.

'We can tidy up later, I'm not in the mood now,' Lucy said as she poured boiling water over the teabag in Mum's cup. Looking at those empties makes you guess who's been here, doesn't it, Georgia?'

'Yes,' I said sadly when I thought of those people I never wanted to be near again.

'I'll take Mum's tea in now,' Lucy told me. 'There's plenty of food in the fridge – I guess it'll be me who'll have to get us our dinner. At least that horrible lot don't bother with our food.'

'They seem to prefer drinking and taking drugs,' I said crossly.

I couldn't bring myself to go back in when Lucy took Mum her tea. Instead, I just stood in the doorway while Lucy did her best to wake her up again. 'Come on, Mum, open your eyes! I've got a nice cup of tea for you,' she kept saying until Mum finally stirred and muttered, 'Thank you, darling.' Lucy managed to catch my eye then and I came in reluctantly. Mum struggled to sit up and my sister rather roughly placed a cushion behind her back so she was able to at least sip her drink without spilling any of it.

Did I see guilt in Mum's eyes when she managed to focus enough to look at me, or did I just imagine it? I still don't know, but I like to think it was there. Lucy managed to get us out of the room quickly by saying, 'We've got homework to do, so we'll go upstairs for a while.'

But there was little interest. Mum wasn't capable of asking about our day at school or holding any sort of conversation with us.

'We'll come down later, Mum, and have dinner together,' Lucy added.

A distant smile crept onto our mother's face then, though I guessed she would be back sleeping before we reached the top of the stairs.

'I can't believe she's mixing with those druggies again. After all we've gone through!' Lucy said, looking quite desperate as she plumped herself down on Sid's bed. 'I don't what to do now – except sort out my homework. I can hardly use the state my mother is in as an excuse not to hand it in tomorrow!'

'I know, I've got some to do as well. Don't feel like it, though,' I told her.

The pair of us put our heads down then and worked for a while, not that it stopped us from worrying. I remember how mixed emotions kept flooding my mind. Anger, disappointment, frustration and sadness all came and went. We didn't deserve this – we were just children, how were we going to cope with this way of life?

'Maybe we should go back to Nan's, Lucy,' I said. 'I love Mum, but like Sid, I don't want to be around those people Mum calls friends.'

I now understood why my brother had left. I remembered him trying to persuade us to go with him and one of his main reasons was that he thought those people were quite frightening.

'Let's just put up with it for it for a while. I'm scared of leaving her alone – I hate to think what those people might encourage her to do. I'm so angry with her; she was really trying too. It's them, Georgia, they must have persuaded her.'

For the next few weeks there were days when Mum tried her best to look bright and fresh. Not that the house ever looked as clean and tidy as when we first moved in. There were a few times when she told us that Nan had been over and others when she talked away to us on our return home.

Of course, we hoped it was a sign that she would stay like that, but by then we knew she probably wouldn't. It was during this time that Sid went out of his way to talk to us.

19

Sid, who often came up to talk with us on our breaks from lessons, asked if Lucy and I would like to meet up after school. 'There's a cafe I think you'd like to go to, before you make your way back home,' he told us. 'It would be good to chat with you both when there's no one else around. We haven't had that much time together in ages, have we?'

I felt like saying, 'not since you decided to leave our home,' but I held back.

'We see each other here every day, don't we?' said Lucy.

'I know, but we can't talk that much in Georgia's part of the playground, can we?'

'I suppose not,' I said.

Glancing at Lucy, I could tell she was a little suspicious as to what was motivating his suggestion: 'What exactly do you want to talk about, Sid?' she wanted to know.

'Oh, come on, Lucy! We only see each other for a few minutes after school or when you come round to Nan's. Not that you come over that often. There are times when I really miss you two. That's why I think it would be really nice for us three to spend more time together, don't you?'

Lucy could hardly argue about that. As for me, not only was my mouth watering at the idea of decent cakes, but also I really wanted to delay going home and the prospect of having some cheerful conversation with my big brother was very appealing. When Lucy and I began the walk home every day, we couldn't stop ourselves from feeling apprehensive. Which mother would be there? Would it be the nice, cheerful one, or the one lying around in a stupor with little or no interest in us.

'So, what's the cafe like, Sid?' I asked.

'Great! You'll love going there. It was Grandad who found it. He's taken me there a couple of times and he loves their cakes. He said they were the best ones he'd ever eaten and then he told me not to tell Nan he said that.'

Lucy and I couldn't help but giggle. Nan knew her cakes were good, but she would hate Grandad being disloyal.

'So, come with me and you can try them and then tell me what you think.'

'I haven't any money on me and neither has Georgia,' Lucy said.

'Don't worry, I have and I want to treat you – after all, you're my sisters. Now, what do you think, Georgia? Wouldn't you like a nice piece of cake?'

The word 'cake' made my eyes sparkle: 'Yes, I'll come.'

'I will too,' Lucy told him. 'I'm not going to walk home on my own while Georgia's stuffing her face with my share of cakes! How far is it from here?'

'It's a five-minute walk, that's all.'

'That's not too bad then. I like cakes as well,' she said, giving him a friendly smile. After all, before our brother left home, Lucy had been very close to him and, like me, she often wished he was still living with us.

'We'll meet at the gates when school finishes. See you both then,' said Sid as he began the walk towards the senior part of the school.

When I had finished my lunch and gone out into the playground, Lucy must have followed me for within seconds she was by my side. From the expression on her face, I could tell she wanted to say something to me before we met up with our brother.

'I'm pretty sure that Nan has asked him to talk to us,' she began. Which told me I was right. 'Maybe she thought we would be more honest with him about what was going on at home. I think that both Nan and Grandad are aware that Mum's back on drugs and if Sid has been told that, then he's going to try and persuade us to move into Nan's. I reckon she gave him enough money to take us out, so we might as well eat as much as we can.'

'Lucy, I think Sid would talk to Grandad more than he would Nan. I wonder if he's told him about Bill and those women.'

'Maybe, but then Sid doesn't know they're back. He's convinced that Bill is a dealer and he would hate the fact that drugs were being brought round to the house for her. Dealers never want addicts to recover, it's bad for business,' Lucy said in a very knowing voice.

I remembered how upset Sid was after Mum was taken

into hospital. He would do anything to get those awful people to leave our mother alone.

'But Lucy, how would our grandparents know about Mum being back on drugs again? She's pretty careful about how she looks when we're invited to their house or when Nan's coming over.'

'You mean when we go over and Sid's always out with his friends. He's still sticking to not wanting to be round her. OK, she can look pretty normal when we go, but Nan's no fool. Don't forget they wanted her to go to rehab so they'll be keeping an eye on her to see if she's kept her promise, so maybe they've given Sid the job of finding out from us what she's really up to. We've got to be so careful about what we say when we go to the cafe.'

At the end of school, we met up with Sid, who looked very pleased that we were going out to tea with him. He chatted a little about what he had done in class as we walked together. And he was right about the cafe. With its rattan chairs lined with pink gingham cushions and deep-pink flowers in tiny vases on each table, we both thought it looked pretty. Sid ordered us all soft drinks and asked if we wanted some scones with jam and cream first, before we ate a slice of cake. We both said yes to that and tucked into them as soon as they arrived at the table.

'Yummy, just out of the oven,' Lucy told him appreciatively, a spot of cream still on her nose.

Sid managed to keep up a light conversation until he came to the subject Lucy had expected him to bring up. First, he praised his way of life with our grandparents and told us how peaceful it was in their home – 'So easy to study for my exams there – Nan won't let me do much work in the house except to bring down my washing and make my bed. How about you two? Is it the same for you?'

'More or less,' Lucy replied quickly, which gained her a somewhat sardonic smile.

It was then he asked us a direct question that we were not prepared for: 'So, how do you feel about her taking drugs again?'

'Seeing as you have nothing to do with her, what makes you think she's doing drugs again?' Lucy asked.

'You might not want to believe this, but our grandparents do know about it and they're concerned about you. It was Grandad who told me, even when we were all at home together.'

Those words shook us. How on earth had they found out? Lucy and I couldn't work it out.

'I know it's true and you've been keeping quiet to protect Mum, so don't even bother denying it. The harm that drugs cause will rub off on you two if they haven't already. There'll be people in the house you should never have to meet. You know that's one of the reasons I left. None of us should have to watch the results of drugs which will make our mother go downhill. That's why I'm here trying to tell you that your life would be better at Nan's.'

'You've said that before, Sid.'

'I did, Lucy, and I meant it. I wanted you to come with me when I left and, in case you haven't noticed, I'm a much happier person than I was before. My marks at school are much higher as well. That's because I have nothing to worry about at Nan's. At weekends they encourage me to meet up with friends and I can bring them back to the house with me any time. I bet you two can't risk doing that. You must be on edge every time you walk home from school. Don't tell me you're not bothered by what you might walk into. I've seen the expressions on your faces when you leave and I can tell that you're both apprehensive, if not scared.'

'Not scared exactly,' said Lucy, 'just concerned about her.'

'OK, I get the hang of that feeling. I promise it's not that I don't care about Mum – in fact, I really miss the mum she used to be. The moment I heard that she was coming out of hospital I couldn't stop hoping that she would agree to go to rehab as Nan was going to offer to pay for it. Not just for her sake, but for ours too. I rushed back from school like you two and waited to hear what Clare and Nan would have to say. As soon as I saw Clare's face, I knew Mum hadn't agreed. I wish she had – don't you, honestly?'

'Then we didn't mind that much, but now we try not to think about her refusing to go,' Lucy said dismally.

I noticed her defences had now come down and she was speaking from the heart.

'I try to do the same,' said Sid. 'When I was told about her being rushed to the hospital, I had thoughts and memories of her running through my head all day at school. And when I was told she was going to get better, I just wanted to hear that she was going back to being the caring mother all three of us loved.'

'Were you told about the promises she made to us all?' Lucy asked.

'Yes, Clare told me. Of course, I hoped they would not be broken but it was obvious to me that neither Nan nor Grandad felt that she would be able to stick to them, nor did Clare. It's so sad that we were all right, isn't it?'

We couldn't help but agree, having banked on her sticking to her promises. Once they were broken, we were so despondent. We had seen how Clare was annoyed about her not getting that treatment. She, too, was sad that her sister might destroy her life. Of course, Nan had been keeping an eye on Mum.

'Nan asked you to talk to us, didn't she? That's why you have the money to pay for us,' said Lucy.

'She did, yes, but that's not the only reason we're here. Honestly, Lucy, I really did want to spend some time with you both. I really worry about you and Georgia. It's not just your grandparents who want you to have a better life, it's me as well. I expect you believed Mum when she promised you.'

'Yes,' said Lucy, her voice full of sadness, 'we did and I think Mum believed herself as well – for a while, anyhow.'

'I think so too. She must have wanted to stick to her promises, but she just couldn't, could she? Now, will you two leave and come and live with Nan?' he persisted.

I almost felt like crying as I listened to Sid, for I could tell that he was being sincere. I didn't say a word as I waited to hear what Lucy was going to say. Would she tell Sid she wanted us to leave home or not? Even after all these years, I'm still not sure what it was I wanted her to say.

Her answer was, 'Not yet.'

'All right, I'm not going to argue with you, Lucy. But I think there'll come a day when you feel you have no other choice but to leave that house. All you need to do then is speak to Nan and she'll help you pack up and move into her home,' Sid told her.

What Lucy told me later as we were walking home was the reason why she had not agreed to leave. She believed that, if Mum was left in the house alone, those people who encouraged her to take drugs would be round even more. 'I hate to think of her habit getting worse,' Lucy said. 'At least with us there, she has days when she does her best to look good and spend time with us.'

What neither of us realised then was that, without professional help, an addict will not try and be careful about how much they take. It's an illness, one that is hard to recover from. Or to be precise, it can be even harder to want to recover. Over the time we stayed with Mum, we watched her descent with great sadness.

20

During the months ahead, I kept thinking that, had we taken Sid's advice, our lives would have been so much more peaceful. Could I cope without Mum in my life? was a question I asked myself more than once. There were times when I truly believed I could. Coming home from school to find the sort of people who Mum called her friends was just one reason I wished I wasn't there.

On the other hand, like so many children whose childhoods had little security, we still refused to break that bond between parent and self. That bond between mother and child is imprinted from the moment they are first held. I suppose it was partly that and the good memories we had of her that made us care so deeply for our mother. Looking back, I can remember being happy on the days when she was her normal self, kind, bright and intelligent. But then like a ghost, she disappeared to be replaced by someone completely different.

There were still days when the real mother appeared, which meant we had a dinner together that Lucy had not cooked and the three of us chatted away. Those days made us happy, although we were by now aware that our happiness was transient and in a couple of days the other mother would take over again. When that one was in the house, we had a mother who was either sitting with the weird group of people we so hated being in our home or lying on the sofa with the glazed look we had become so used to. I suppose the reason I never stopped loving her was because the picture of my real mother has stayed in my mind right up until today.

Lucy and I both sighed with exasperation and disappointment on the days when we came back from school to find the house in a mess: the odd splattering of blood on the walls, empty syringes in the bin or by the side of the sofa, a pile of dirty dishes and glasses in the kitchen. We had a shrewd idea who had been there and what they had all been up to. At least they were gone before we got there, which gave us something to be grateful for. Needless to say, on those days Mum was either lying on the sofa or had made her way upstairs only to pass out on her bed. Whatever it was, we preferred washing up and cleaning the kitchen to having to meet Bill and those dreadful women.

There were times, though, when we were unable to avoid them. We would come back from school and there would be Bill with the group of junkies, which was growing larger each time we came across them. They must have only just arrived for the kitchen was still as tidy as when we left in the morning. We would grab some food and then shoot upstairs, where we stayed until we heard them leave.

21

Over the coming months, Mum's condition became worse. There were mornings when she had stayed in bed and we didn't see her until we returned from school. Sid had been right about us always being worried about the state that she would be in when we got home. I don't think that either of us knew what to do. Lucy was back to cooking our dinner almost every night, as she had our breakfast, when Mum was still in bed.

By then, I had become a very emotionally messed-up little girl. I had these strange habits of shaking my hands, making choking noises with my throat and blinking my eyes. I understand now that it was anxiety that was causing it. Hardly surprising, I suppose.

I had come to the point when I had to accept that my life was far from normal. Other children I knew at school would talk about what they did at the weekend. Simple things such as going out with their parents, seeing a film, having dinner where their mother had cooked their favourite meal and being taken shopping to buy some new clothes and having tea out. All those normal things that parents do with their children. There was little of that happening for us.

Our school friends would not have understood one word if I had told them that I often came home to find a group of drug addicts sitting around our home. Did any of them have mothers who fell asleep with a lit cigarette in their hand? Would they have to go and take it from them and put it out before it singed the bedding or the furniture? I'm sure that none of them had ever came home to find their mum comatose on the floor, a syringe and a rubber strap beside her.

Those were the secrets I had to keep and never talk about.

22

Lucy and I couldn't stand how Mum had stopped being bothered about us meeting those friends of hers. Nor did she care about what we saw after they had been there. She seldom cleaned or tidied the house and we hardly ever had a change of clothes because she never put anything into the washing machine. Bedding could be unchanged for weeks, unless we did it ourselves at the weekend. Yet there were still days when we saw the mother we loved. Then she would get the vacuum out, cook nice dinners and her conversation with us would be, if not always fun, less monosyllabic. Sadly, those happy days became less and less.

Maybe I haven't explained the blood on the walls. All I know, or want to know, is that there are certain ways of getting drugs into the bloodstream quicker. But despite my revulsion, those memories refuse to leave my mind. Some children of addicts become addicts themselves, but I have hated drugs my whole life because of the things I saw.

Lucy and I tried to wash the blood off the walls but

sometimes it wouldn't come off. When Nan visited and saw them, she must have told Grandad to get one of his team over to clean and repaint the walls. They were both so worried about us, especially Grandad. What he had to say to his daughter I don't know – they were always careful that nothing came out in front of us. But then they had no idea of what we already knew.

What I do know now is that my grandparents had found themselves in a terrible position. Nan, noticing our downcast expressions, would ask if we would like to stay with her for a while. As young as we were, we knew she really meant, come and live with us.

'No, we're all right here, Nan,' we kept telling her, which was hardly the truth and I guess she was aware of that. I should think that she worried about us from the moment she was awake. She was unable to push back the thoughts of the damage Mum was doing to us. The only way we could be forced to leave was if she went to social services and explained everything to them. They would have had us out of that house in seconds. Nan must have thought about doing that several times but, had she done so, we would not have been happy about leaving Mum and not only would she lose the love of her daughter, but her granddaughters too. Nan would have ended up with two resentful girls in her house and one extremely upset daughter in another.

I know now that my nan was completely aware of what went on in our home but had no idea of the danger we were in or just what we were witnessing daily. She tried asking us the odd question, which was a waste of time because we didn't tell her anything until we had no other choice. There were, however, an increasing number of times when I felt I couldn't stand being in our house.

One day we arrived home and the living room was full of random people but no one even looked up at us. Clouds of smoke were drifting above their heads and, leaning towards Lucy, I whispered, 'It stinks of rotten eggs.' She had a job not to laugh out loud and instead just gripped my arm and said, 'Upstairs now.'

A few minutes later, she came up with some orange juice and a couple of sandwiches: 'We'll stay here till they've gone.'

'Shall we go to Nan's, Lucy? It's getting worse here, isn't it? These people scare me,' I said.

'Let's just put up for it for a while longer. I'm scared of leaving her.'

Lucy's answer was nearly always the same.

Then there would be a day when Mum was bright and chatty, which made me also forget that I wanted to leave.

In the end it was well over a year before Lucy and I both decided that we couldn't take any more. Not just because of Mum's habit, or even the number of people who came round to do drugs, but other situations that began to frighten us. So much so that it disturbed both our sleep and our confidence.

Our fear of what might happen to Mum began when we found some items that completely horrified Lucy. There was a small cupboard in the living room that Mum had told us was where she kept a few personal things, which made Lucy more than curious. She was even more suspicious when she realised that Mum now kept it locked. On one of those Saturday mornings, when Mum was still in bed, she noticed that she had forgotten to take the key out of the lock. The sight of that key meant that there was no way Lucy could resist opening the cupboard. All the colour left her face when she saw what was inside.

I stood near her shoulder peering in as well and for some reason I felt quite fascinated by what I saw. At our ages, nine and twelve, we should have been more puzzled, but Lucy knew straight away what each item was. It took her a while to explain to me what she thought. The cupboard was full of asthma pumps, small glass pipes, packets of foil, elastic bands, needles and, finally, a piece of fabric, which Lucy pulled out so that she could see the small dark lumps it was wrapped around. With a loud sigh she wrapped it up again and shoved it back in the cupboard. I can't remember the other things there, but as Lucy told me, there was just about everything for different types of drug addiction.

'What do they do with the asthma pump?' I asked, wondering if someone had a breathing problem and needed it.

'It makes them get even higher. I read about it.' She sighed again, more deeply this time as if her heart was breaking, and then she slammed the door shut, locked it and threw the key on the coffee table. I could tell that she was really distressed.

'Mum's going to end up in hospital again,' she said bleakly. 'I wonder if this time she'll ever come out.'

'Don't say that, Lucy.'

'I know, I can hardly believe that Mum's slipping away from us. If that cupboard is ever left open again, don't touch it. Filthy hands will have been all over every piece in there,' she warned.

That was the beginning of me having more unhappy thoughts about what was happening in our home; thoughts that turned into nightmares when I was asleep. In my dreams I saw people rolling their eyes and looking crazy while on the floor was my mother. Her face was the younger, peaceful one I remembered from before we left Dad. Crouched around her were the people we disliked seeing, laughing and mocking her.

I began to believe then that those nightmares were sending me messages. Hadn't I heard a voice telling me to get away in my dreams? *Those people that your mum allows in your home are a danger to you*, it kept telling me. *Look at your brother, see how healthy and happy he looks.*

A picture of the inside of the cupboard then came into my dream and, as my hands moved towards the contents, I woke screaming and sobbing with my head spinning. At school I could hardly hear what the teacher was saying; it was the voice I kept hearing instead.

I think it was then that the twitching started.

23

As I write my story, I have become aware that a few of my childhood memories have vanished. From what I have learnt from Sid and Lucy, they were the ones that my subconscious could not cope with. There are some, though, that lie dormant and then suddenly emerge to all so vividly remind me of my childhood pain.

At that time in my life, when I was only nine, I had begun to dislike weekends intensely. My mother had changed so much that school had become Lucy's and my escape route. We never knew what to expect when we walked home after our classes were finished. Where once we would have rushed, now the apprehension weighed us down and we walked with leaden footfalls. Sometimes the house was invaded by druggies, and on other increasingly rare occasions, it was quiet and our mother appeared normal. As time went by, we were both beginning to think that a move to Nan's house might be preferable. It only took a few more weeks of one or both of our parents making the situation unbearable for the level of trauma to increase. Being scared and upset was becoming the norm.

The first time was when Mum managed to make me cry. The final straw was a situation that arose in the house that was so frightening, it made me freeze with terror. That was enough, I could not stay there for one night more.

It was the afternoon that I had taken a picture which I had drawn in my art class home to Mum as a present. I had asked the teacher if I could take it home with me and he had agreed. I had taken some photos to school to help me and one of them showed the three of us standing with Mum, who was smiling confidently into the lens – I decided to base my artwork on that photo.

I doubt if the people in my painting were entirely recognisable, but as the teacher was generous with his praise, I was quite excited. When school was finished and I met Lucy near the gate, I showed it to her straight away.

'Can you see yourself in it?' I asked excitedly.

'I can, and I think your picture is wonderful, Georgia,' she told me.

'I'm giving it to Mum as soon as we get home. I hope she'll be pleased with it. The teacher wants my next one to be done as well as this one so he can pin it on the wall for everyone to see.'

'I'm sure Mum will love it,' said Lucy, placing an arm around my shoulder. 'Let's hope it will be just us in the house with her and no visitors.'

'I hope not. I want her to put my drawing on the wall. Do you think she will?'

'Of course I do, but leave showing it to her if those people are there,' my sister warned.

What a shame that was the one sentence I ignored. I was so looking forward to giving the picture to Mum and thinking it would make her happy that for once in a long time I was walking home with anticipation.

We were both disappointed when we opened the door and heard loud voices. As we couldn't stand the smirks and odd comments, we usually went straight upstairs to our room. Lucy sometimes took herself into the kitchen to get us a soft drink and a sandwich and then came up and worked at Sid's desk.

This time I refused to let those visitors stop me from giving Mum her present. After all, this was our home not theirs and I could go where I wanted, which was the living room. Lucy tried to stop me going in: 'Just wait till they've gone.'

'But I want to give it to Mum now,' my nine-year-old self protested stubbornly.

'Mummy, Mummy, look what I made you at school!' I said loudly when I went into the living room. I was so pleased with myself and my achievement that I expected praise from her.

'Get out, go to your room!' she screamed without even taking a glance at the picture I was trying to hand over to her.

That was enough to make me run out of the room and then, thinking of the smirks on some of those people's faces, I burst into tears. Lucy kept telling me it was because of whatever stuff Mum had taken that day – 'Come on, Georgia, you know that's not our real mum! She would never shout at you like that – it's the drugs that turn her into someone different. It's best to leave her alone when she's with those horrible people, it's their fault that Mum keeps taking stuff that's so bad for her. I know they bring whatever it is over to her.'

It was only a few days later that Mum shocked us both so much that Lucy was just as tearful as I had been.

24

The second upsetting incident was caused by Dad. I was waiting outside in the garden for him one Saturday morning and I must have been out there for nearly two hours before he eventually arrived. Naturally, it upset me that he had not bothered to arrive on time or let Mum know he was running late. That might not sound too bad, except it was drizzling with rain and, having made myself look really nice, I was getting soaked and I was bedraggled. Yes, I could have gone back in, but then I would have to listen to Mum, who in the mood she was in, would have not stopped complaining about him. I just didn't want to have my ears filled with her running him down.

When Dad eventually turned up, I tried not to show that I was fed up about having to wait so long. Still, I was pleased to see him finally arriving. He pushed open the passenger door and called out, 'In you get, Georgia!' Shivering a little, I climbed in as fast as I could. Just as I was clicking on my seat belt, Dad leant over to give me a kiss on the cheek.

It was then I smelt the alcohol on his breath, and almost at the same time, the car plunged forward. Between the car jumping and the alcohol smell, I had the horrible feeling that he was not completely sober. He started talking and then I realised that his voice was slurring, which made me feel even more alarmed.

If I had known the reason he was so late was because he had been drinking all day with his brother, I would have made up some sort of excuse not to go out with him. That day I quickly learnt how alcohol can turn a pleasant man into a bad-tempered one who becomes angry at the slightest thing. Being with him that day and a couple of others made me wonder how many drinks it takes to makes a nice person completely disappear. But then I was already used to seeing how that might happen when my mother took drugs.

All the time I spent in the car frightened me. Instead of keeping his eyes on the road, Dad kept turning his head in my direction to give me some feeble excuses about being late. 'Sorry I made you wait,' he slurred, 'I was with my brother, we were celebrating.' Not that he told me what the occasion was. My heart sank when I heard who he had been with, for his brother Simon was a man with a terrible reputation. From what I had heard, he had an uncontrollable and violent temper. He was seen by a lot of people as being a walking disaster, especially as when someone annoyed him in particular, he did not hesitate to take a gun out. Evidently, he had done this more than once.

Rumour had it that Dad's brother had gone to a pub with a gun. He had fired it at the ceiling, not at the person. But the noise and the threat of it was terrible. His intention, which he succeeded at, was to make everyone in there shake with fright. How he wasn't arrested, I don't know. Maybe it was because most of the customers in there didn't want to meet any of the boys in blue. At least that was what I'd heard anyhow. Simon was certainly not an uncle I wanted anything to do with.

I could tell that his effect on Dad was not a good one. From what my father said, Uncle Simon had been running Mum down so much, Dad's rage began simmering over.

'Georgia, how dare your mum not invite me in to see my girls? Just look at you, you're soaking wet!' he said. 'Don't you agree that I should be able to come into the house?'

I was too busy gripping my seat belt tightly and thought it best not to reply to those sorts of questions. All the while I kept telling myself not to be so frightened. I might not have been if I hadn't heard my grandparents saying numerous times how dangerous drunk drivers could be. Remembering that, I couldn't stop myself from asking him to slow down a little. That was enough for him to turn his head towards me again and glare.

'Don't be silly, Georgia! I'm not going fast, so don't make a fuss,' he said as his foot went down on the pedal even harder and the car surged forward. That was when I remembered that he had never liked being told what to do.

I can still picture that frightening drive and the place we went for something to eat. It was a pub that had a small restaurant at the back. But I can't remember what I ate, although in retrospect, I can almost hear him ordering the drinks that he kept knocking back. He must have known that worried me and it was as if he was doing it on purpose. By the expression on his face when he looked at me over the top of his glass, I could tell it was his way of letting me know that I wasn't to say one word about it.

I knew there were going to be questions coming in my direction and I felt my stomach clench as I waited for the inevitable. It didn't take him long to tell me that he knew why Mum had been in hospital. Now, I would probably say that it was a guess and he wanted to trick me into telling him the truth.

'She'd taken too many drugs, hadn't she, Georgia?'

'I don't think so,' was my answer, as I hoped he would stop there. I prayed he wasn't going to bring up similar questions to the ones he'd fired at Lucy a while ago.

'How many drugs is your mum taking now? Is she using heroin yet?' he wanted to know.

I must have mumbled something like I hadn't seen her take anything, which was more or less true. Even though both Lucy and I were totally aware that this was what she did behind our backs. I expect my cheeks went red as I tried my best not to give Dad the answer he wanted – I wished I was as good as Lucy was at keeping a blank face.

'Oh, come off it, Georgia! I found out why she was in hospital. I know she nearly died. Better for all of you if she had, though, then I would have the right to take you and Lucy away from her.'

Oh, not that again, I thought, as I tried to calm down and spoon some ice cream into my mouth. I was too scared to tell him that, whatever happened, I wouldn't want to stay with him. I could imagine that brother of his bursting in whenever he felt like it. He might have been my uncle, but I never wanted to be around him.

'Don't know why your grandparents don't just have you removed by social services and then handed over to me,' he kept saying.

I didn't tell him that wasn't their idea at all – it was us moving in with them that they wanted. In fact, Dad's name was hardly mentioned. At least not then, although later on it was, but hardly in a good way.

When I had to get in the car to be driven home, I must have clung to my seat belt all the way. My body was braced against the seat and I kept expecting him to crash the car.

It was certainly a day without much enjoyment.

I was so relieved when I got home in one piece. But if I had thought that day was a disappointment, there were a couple of others that were much worse coming along fairly soon.

25

When I was upstairs with Lucy, I told her about Dad's bad driving, the drinking and the questions he threw at me while he was knocking back more drinks.

'Good thing you've not got to see him next weekend,' Lucy said.

'Depends on what happens here,' I replied, trying my best to grin.

Luckily for me, the next few days with Mum were not too bad. Lucy and I breathed a sigh of relief when we came home to find it was only her there. I had heard her on the phone saying, 'Oh, you're going up north, are you?' My guess was it was Bill she was talking to then because we didn't see him for a while.

'Maybe those women are running the business while Bill's away. Or perhaps they've just found another place to sit around and get drugged out of their heads in,' Lucy said.

I still have some happy memories about Mum at that time, even when her willpower had mostly disappeared.

Over the last weeks of living with her, I can't say that there weren't a few good times that I've never forgotten. The one I like remembering the most might sound peculiar, but for some reason it still manages to make me laugh. Mum would disappear into the toilet for ages. Upset tummy was her excuse, but however young I was, I knew what she was up to: she wanted privacy to put a needle in her arm and feel whatever drug it was coursing through her body. All her worries would leave her then and make her life seem more exciting. To be fair, she probably didn't want her children seeing her injecting herself either. But then perhaps she didn't think that we already knew what was taking place in there.

It was a Saturday morning when Lucy had gone out to meet some friends. I was in the house alone with Mum when I saw her scuttling into the toilet. After waiting a short while, I lay down flat on the floor so that I could look under the door. There she was, her arm still attached to the syringe that her fingers were curled round. I winced as she injected herself, but I still managed to watch. I waited till she finished pushing the stuff in and then called out under the door that I knew what she was doing and I'd tell Nan what was going on.

Instead of arguing, she ignored me and began to sing. It was a song she had once written herself, before the drugs took away all her creative skills. I loved it when she used to sing to us, but that morning, the part of the song she had written was sung in a thin but beautiful voice: 'Mum was cooking bread, she wore a dirty red rag around her head.' I wish I could remember all the words of that song. I have several notebooks still with her poetry in them, but I never found that one.

I didn't call Nan, not then. Instead, I just sat there on the floor for ages, waiting for her to come out. When she did, she was in a dreamlike state and bent down and ruffled my hair. Somehow, both of us managed to laugh.

I think that was just about the last time we were able to do that together.

26

I had a phone call from Dad about a week later, asking me if I wanted to go out with him again. If his voice hadn't been slurry again, I might have said yes, but the thought of climbing into that car with him driving so badly made me make up an excuse not to go out with him.

'We're going to Nan's in a while,' I told him.

'All of you?' he asked.

'Just Lucy and I,' I said quickly.

What I didn't know then was the reason that he asked me that question. My quickly invented answer turned out to be a huge mistake. If only I had said all three of us, instead of telling him it was just Lucy and I who were leaving the house, our day might have remained peaceful. Unfortunately, Lucy had gone out to do some shopping for Mum and was then going round to a friend's house.

It was a warm, sunny day and I was happy enough to be in the house with Mum. I went outside for a while to play with a swingball and then I heard a car pulling up in front of the house. Hoping it might be Clare, I looked up and recognised Dad's black Audi. To my horror, I saw it wasn't just Dad who was climbing out of it, but also his brother, Simon. Neither of them looked in my direction as they were staring at the house. As I had lied about going to Nan's, they were not expecting anyone to be in the garden. Should I run into the house and warn Mum? I wondered. I was so scared, I nearly froze and came very close to wetting myself. The moment I saw that thickset thug of an uncle with those enormous muscular arms, I knew there was going to be real trouble. I ran in screaming as loud as I could, telling Mum to lock the door, but they came up behind me, gave me a shove and barged past me. I heard Mum screaming at them to get out and Simon shouting, 'No way, you pathetic, miserable bitch!'

I stood by the door shaking and heard her crying out for them to stop each time their fists slammed into her body. They didn't stop straight away, though – I think what they wanted more than hurting her was to have her completely humiliated in front of the neighbours. She was only half-dressed when they dragged her out of the house, threw her down on the path and repeatedly kicked her as they called her a 'fucking junkie'.

I was screaming and sobbing hysterically when the neighbours started opening their doors to see what all the commotion was about.

'She's a junkie bitch!' Dad shouted so they could hear him. 'She's a terrible mother, I'm going to get my children away from her.'

One look at Simon stopped any neighbour from

tackling them and, in full view, he took aim and kicked my mother in her now exposed ribs. I kept screaming for help, begging them to leave her alone, and as Simon aimed another kick, I tried to stop him but he just grinned and shoved me out of the way with one hand while his boot went into Mum again.

That was enough for the neighbours to begin shouting at them. One of them – Jean – rushed inside to phone Grandad.

'Her father's coming, he's called the police,' she shouted at them. She held up her phone and took photos and a video. 'I've got photos of you two, I'll show the police. You'll be in trouble then.'

'He only wants to get his kids back from this junkie,' Simon yelled in return. Simon laughed at them all with their cameras out but he and Dad, satisfied that Mum was hurt enough, walked to the car.

Jean came over and helped get Mum back into the house. 'Your grandad will be here soon, Georgia,' she told me. As she got Mum onto the sofa, I heard her say that he would make sure she would be all right.

A few minutes later, Grandad arrived with Clare. Jean just said, 'I'd better leave now, but phone me if you need any help – I filmed a lot of it on my phone.'

Clare was examining all the bruises and told Grandad to take me into the kitchen and get Mum a very sweet tea. Grandad tried to comfort me as best he could. I could tell that he was shaken and also very angry at what had taken place in our home. He sat down while the kettle was boiling, pulled me towards him and gave me a huge hug. I leant against his shoulder and he gently wiped the tears from my face. After a while, when he felt that not just my tears had stopped but also the fear, he told me softly that nothing like that would ever happen again.

'I'm going to make sure that you're all safe here. I won't have you being frightened like that, nor will I allow anyone to hurt your mother like that again. Do you know what a restraining order is, Georgia? It means that, once it's issued by a court, both your father and that loutish brother of his will be forbidden by the law from coming anywhere near this house. They would be arrested if they did. I'm going to tell your neighbours the same thing, so if they see either him or his brother again, they can call the police. It's a good thing you have Jean as a neighbour – I've done work on her house, which is why she has my phone number. I'm sure if I asked her, she would ring the police as well as me if she ever saw one of them nearby.'

Grandad made it all sound easy. What he didn't tell me was that he would have to get an emergency order, which would last until a court case. It would be up to him to make sure that, once it was issued, Dad and his brother would know about it. I listened to what he was saying and, when it sank in, I realised that I wouldn't be going out with Dad again. Anyhow, I wouldn't want to after what he'd just done. I had now seen him twice being bad-tempered and scary but it was when I looked down at my bracelet that I remembered the nice times we had had together and the tears welled in my eyes.

I can understand why I felt I would miss him then. Young

children who end up in care often still find it difficult to have a parent disappear from their lives. Though Dad wasn't completely gone from mine. I saw him twice more and each time he broke the law. After the second time, he disappeared.

27

Dad did something that few people would believe he could be so stupid as to get involved in. From what I've been told, it was when he first knew about the emergency restraining order. If that made him angry, I should think his brother went completely berserk. The two of them would have got more and more wound up until they decided there was only one thing to do: get Grandad to cancel the order.

I can imagine now those two pacing up and down, fists clenched in fury, swearing away. They would both have known all the risks of coming near us again. And who did they think had arranged it? For a few seconds Dad might have thought that Mum had before realising that it was her father and, as far as he was concerned, it had to be sorted out. Not being able to drive to our home to pick me or Lucy up made him even more angry. By then he had become convinced that he would give the court all the reasons he could think of for Lucy and I to live with him. After all, it was not him who had left Mum, it was she who had taken all of us away from the family home. If that wasn't bad enough, she was an addict, which he was certain could be proved, and we would be handed over to him. But not when there was a restraining order in place, so that had to be got rid of.

That was all he thought of, not how, after Mum left him, he had conned her and Grandad out of a lot of money. He should have blamed himself, for what possible excuse could he have had for his actions in our home? It was unlikely that he gave any thought to his own crimes. Drunk driving, beating up a woman and property theft among them. He just didn't seem to understand that none of us wanted to live with him. I must have been the only one who was still a little fond of him, as odd as that may sound. I had enjoyed being with him when he was in a good mood but being with him could also be unpredictable and scary; as for his brother, he made me shudder.

28

It was a Sunday morning when Mum received a call from Dad. It was a good thing she didn't slam down the phone before she heard what he had to say. He told her that he was going to see her parents and try to get some sense into them. He was going to tell social services that Mum was on drugs, which meant they could take us away from the family. After all, he said, Grandad knew about it and allowed us to stay there – 'I'm not putting up with what he's done to stop me taking Georgia out. I know she likes coming out with me.' Mum was shaking at the anger in his voice but plucked up the courage to say, 'Then you shouldn't have done what you did to me,' before hanging up.

I didn't know about the call, but Mum explained it to us all later. It was a good thing that it was one of those days when she appeared to be looking healthy and wide awake. Otherwise, there might have been a huge calamity.

'Let's get in the car and go for a drive,' Mum said after she had composed herself. She must have wanted to find out what

Dad and his brother were up to – she knew her parents' house was empty as they had gone out for lunch and Sid, as usual, was spending the day with friends. Dad and his brother would more than likely expect them to be in. Lunchtime would have been a good time to get there as Nan always made a big Sunday lunch and they wanted to surprise them – or perhaps shock them would be the better way of putting it.

It was my turn to sit in the front of the car that day and I knew the route and where it took us.

'Are we going to Nan and Grandad for lunch?'

'No, Georgia, they're out – I'm just going to drop something there,' she told me and pulled up a little way from the house so that she could watch it without being seen.

She had guessed right, although what we saw was a lot worse than she had expected. It made us all gasp, for there was Dad climbing out of the Audi with his brother, who was holding a shotgun.

'Head down, Georgia,' she told me as, with my mouth wide open with amazement, I was sitting forward and peering out of the window. Mum's foot pressed down on the accelerator as she sped off without them spotting us.

'They're going to break in,' Mum said calmly. 'Foolish villains, those two. Here's the police station. You two stay in the car, I'll only be a couple of minutes.'

As she was walking out again, some policemen came out and jumped into their cars.

'Let's follow them and watch the fun,' she told us. 'Nan and Grandad are on their way back now – I got the police to phone the restaurant. Better them telling them than me.

The police don't want us too near the house, not when guns are about. But we can park in that road before it's blocked and then we'll see what's happening.'

We got there before Nan and Grandad arrived and we could see that the police were outside of the house and the road was being closed. All we knew was what the police told Mum later. They tried to stop Grandad from entering. 'It's my house and I'm going in,' he told them. And in he went. As the police weren't armed, they were waiting for the riot police to arrive. Grandad didn't want Dad or his brother pointing that gun at the police and firing.

We never did learn how Grandad managed to stop everything. He must have told Dad and Simon that he could get them out of the house without being shot or charges being laid. He wouldn't have cared less about the brother, but he didn't want my father to be harmed badly. He must have told the police a few lies, such as the guns weren't loaded and they were just playing at being nasty. Maybe he took the ammunition out himself, but after Dad and Simon were taken off to the police station, they never had to go to court.

29

On the morning I came down with painful stomach cramps and a high temperature, Mum was thankfully having one of her bright and normal days. As I might have something that made me contagious, she didn't want Lucy also catching it, so she phoned Nan. She told her about my symptoms and asked if she would mind picking Lucy up from school and have her stay the night. Mum said then that, if I didn't seem any better by midday, she would take me to our local doctor's afternoon surgery.

But my cramps became even more painful and I was beginning to feel cold and shivery. Noticing how flushed my face was, Mum asked me to open my mouth wide as she popped a thermometer into it. I watched her face as she removed it and, when she realised how high my temperature had climbed, she made a call to 999 and asked for the ambulance service. The person on the other end told her it would be dispatched immediately so that I could be examined by the paramedic and, if necessary, taken into the hospital.

Just to give Mum more problems, Dad managed to get into the house. She had me tucked up on the sofa and was trying to give me plenty of iced squash to bring my temperature down, apparently. They seemed to help my stomach too and, looking back on that day, I must have kept falling in and out of sleep, which might be the reason why my memory is hazy. But I do remember Dad shouting and hearing another man's voice telling him to leave the house. But there's one picture that hasn't disappeared. It's me looking up at Mum from my prone position on the settee and seeing the terror in her huge blue eyes.

After I had recovered, I asked Mum if those vague memories were real, or just part of a bad nightmare. She grimaced then and told me that it was not a dream, it all happened – 'The nightmare was a living one, which your dad brought with him.'

'How did he get in? I seem to remember he was on the phone, that's all.'

'Yes, you were in the living room half-asleep or maybe half-conscious. Your body was so hot then and I didn't want to leave you alone for even a minute until the medics arrived. He just wouldn't listen when I tried to explain it to him. I told him I was worried that it was peritonitis and I was waiting for the ambulance. He just refused to accept that you were ill and tried to persuade me to get you on the phone. I told him that this was not the right time. Your dad, being the person he is, began singing down the line as loudly as he could, "Georgia On My Mind" – I suppose he was hoping you would hear him.'

'I didn't, though.'

'Just as well – he was so completely flat and slurring so badly. I finished the call by telling him I had to go back to you and I hung up before he could say another word. You were lying on the sofa with your eyes shut so I don't think you heard much of the conversation. I just wish I hadn't told him what I was waiting for. He might have been drunk, but he was cunning enough to know that, if I thought the medics had arrived at the door, I would open it as fast as I could – that's how he got in. Though, of course, I had no idea that he was so close to the house when he called. Drunk as he was, he was smart enough to wait for a short while before he knocked on the door. Silly me, of course, I should have looked out the window to see who it was. But then I was expecting the ambulance and just thought they had got here very quickly, so I opened the door without checking.

'There he was, leaning on the door frame with a smirk on his face. I begged him to leave, saying I didn't want another scene. Him being there really upset me. I tried as hard as I could to slam that door shut. He just laughed at me and pushed it back and brushed me out of the way as he walked in. 'She's in the living room, isn't she?' he said. In he went to look at you. He didn't seem to notice that I had placed a blanket over you because you were shivering and that your eyes were shut, he just sat down near you.'

'Did he hit you, Mum, or push you away?'

'No, actually I think he was more sad than bad-tempered. The smile he gave when he saw you was soft and affectionate, but also a bit sad. I knew he loved you just by that expression.

Everything had gone wrong with him, he told me, as he looked down at you. Your eyes flickered then, you must have recognised his voice.'

'Did I hear him saying he loved you, Mum?'

Another memory had flashed into my mind.

'Yes, he did, but then he told me he could never be with me again because of the drugs I took.'

That straightforward answer from Mum admitting her addiction has stayed in my mind so clearly. I wish she had remained as honest as that. Not so much with us, but with herself. Had she done so, maybe her future would have been a better one.

'I seem to remember something Dad did. He took hold of my hand and stroked it before he said at least twice, "Georgia, don't you love your daddy? Your mum's a junkie, why do you want to live with her and not me?" Did he say that, Mum?'

'He did, but you didn't answer him, Georgia. Your eyes closed and I think you fell back to sleep. You certainly didn't want to say anything. Funnily enough, you did wake up a few minutes later and that was funny. Your dad was reaching in his back pocket for something and, after the last time and what he had done at my parents' house, it scared me enough to make me squeal with fright. I thought, *he's going to pull out a gun and kill us*. My cry must have got through to you. Do you know what you did?'

'No, Mum, I can't remember,' I said.

'You jumped on his back and bit him! He just pulled you off and gently laid you back down. He wasn't angry

with you, he just tucked the rug around you again and said
you must be having a strange dream to have done that in
your sleep.'

'And what was in his pocket?'

'Nothing dangerous at all. It was his wallet and in it he
had a photo of you. He said that you looked peaceful now
you were asleep again and that you were the child he loved
so much. He seemed almost tearful when he told me how he
missed taking you out with him.'

'I miss him too sometimes, but I don't like what he gets up
to. That scares me.'

'I told him that. I also said that, if he had not mixed with
his brother, who got him doing such crazy things, then more
than likely he would still be able to take you out. I actually felt
sorry for him then.

'It was when the ambulance arrived and he heard the
medics coming through the door that he began to look both
angry and confused. He hadn't noticed that I hadn't closed the
door after he got in. He heard a man's voice calling out my
name and, when I told him it was the ambulance people, can
you guess what he asked me?'

'Did he think a burglar had got in?'

'He asked if it was a boyfriend who I'd given a key to.'

I laughed at that.

'I told him not to be so silly as I got up to go to the hall.
I could tell he was turning angry when he tried to grab hold
of my arm to stop me going. He just didn't seem to take in
what I told him. The way he spoke next just didn't make
any sense. He started telling me that he was not having his

daughter taken anywhere. When I went into the hall, he began his shouting, saying, "I won't let them take you." Those two men didn't seem in the least concerned when they heard him. Maybe he might have heard me telling them as quietly as I could that he was my ex-husband and he had forced his way in. I also whispered the words 'restraining order' and they immediately understood.

'"Don't worry, Mrs Turner, we'll explain everything that's happening, and if she needs to go to the hospital, we will deal with him." They must have thought your dad was the type of person who didn't believe in hospitals, not someone who would physically try and stop them, but then they didn't know your dad.

'They would have changed their minds when they saw him standing in the middle of the room. He looked them up and down and asked who they were and what they were doing there. It's a wonder those medics didn't say something about stating the obvious. Instead, they just told him they were both qualified paramedics and had been sent by the hospital to see if you needed to see a doctor urgently. But unfortunately, nothing they said to your dad penetrated that drunken mind of his.

'It was when he saw one of the men placing his fingers on your wrist to see how your pulse was that he just about screamed with fury. He shouted at that poor man to take his filthy hands off his daughter. If that wasn't enough, when the medic turned round to say something calming to him, he lashed out with his clenched fist and struck the man in the ribs. But your dad should have known that medics who often carry stretchers are pretty strong. The other one got hold of him and wrenched his arms back so hard, he was almost bent double.

'"We are here to take your daughter to hospital because she's very unwell," he told him remarkably coolly. "Her mother's coming to the hospital with her and she will want to lock up when we go. Sir, what's your problem?"

I guess he meant "so you get out". At least that's what your dad thought and another roar came from him. The medic he had attacked said very calmly that, if he didn't go, all he had to do was press a button on his phone to make the police arrive swiftly. I didn't really want him arrested so I reminded him about the restraining order. I told him that the police would arrest him if they found him anywhere near the house. I don't know where I got the courage, Georgia – I just wanted to get you to hospital without his drama. "Just go, Cliff, please," I said. Thankfully, it seemed to work. The one holding him said he would walk him to the door. He asked your dad if he accepted that. He glared a bit but said all right, he would go.'

'And did he go straight away, Mum?'

'He did, thank goodness. Those medics were really kind about it all. They told me it was not the first time they had met a belligerent drunk like him.'

'They put me on the stretcher, didn't they?'

'Yes, when we got to the hospital, they wheeled you in really fast. I was so worried – I had to wait for ages to hear what was wrong with you. All the dreadful illnesses were running through my head, I was so worried about you. I can't tell you how relieved I was when the doctor came and told me it was just a nasty virus but not one of the serious ones, but he wanted to keep you there for a couple of days because you were very dehydrated and they needed to bring your temperature down before you could go home. Even then, you would still have to rest for at least a week.'

'What happened with Dad?'

'Poor sod, he rang me up the next morning to apologise and he was sober. He said he knew he had broken the law and, if I didn't report him to the police, he would leave this area and go up North. He just about begged me to believe him and not report what he had done to the police.'

'What did you say to him?'

'I told him that I didn't want to cause him any trouble and, if he was leaving, I would keep quiet about it. But if I ever saw him near here again, then for all our sakes, I would have to. I also reminded him that Grandad might not be so forgiving.'

Dad kept his promise: he took off to the north of England and I didn't see him again for six years.

* * *

During those days when I was ill, Mum forced herself to reduce her drug taking to next to nothing so that she could be with me. Why couldn't she stick to it? I wondered as I lay in my hospital bed. She brought me in fruit and books to read and during visiting time she sat beside my bed, telling me how much she was looking forward to taking me back home.

Although I was only in there for a few days, I was pleased to leave and I was hopeful that Mum might have got the fright she needed to stay clean. On our return home, she made sure no unwanted visitors appeared in the house and I felt she was doing her utmost to get me feeling better. She cooked delicious food and placed a bowl of fruit near me so I could help myself. She was also good company. When she sat down near me and chattered, it was lovely but tiring and I suggested we watched a film. She popped down to the video shop nearby and hired a video which we could all watch together when Lucy was back from school.

Nan was a frequent visitor and her cakes and biscuits were accompanied by meat pies and soups. She looked pleased to see me beginning to look better. 'Your mum's certainly looking after you well,' she noted. Mum and I were really pleased at this observation.

During my short stay of convalescence, as Mum called it, I felt that she was doing everything to put both Lucy and I first. That feeling of contentment was sadly short-lived, for after I was well enough to go back to school, it seemed in no time at all, our lives went back to how they had been before my illness. I think it only took a couple of weeks for those visitors to start arriving again. The kitchen was stacked up with dirty dishes and glasses and the rest of the house was starting to look neglected again. Within just a few weeks, those visitors were bringing their drugs into the house on an almost daily basis. Then a couple of things happened that left my sister and I with little choice but to move in with our grandparents.

* * *

It had nothing to do with Dad, it was all about what our year teachers had noticed at school. They must have talked about it together and then decided it needed to be discussed with the headteacher. The Head contacted not only Mum, but Nan too. She would have known straight away that there must have been a serious reason for them wanting to see her.

Nan didn't ask for any details on the phone, she just went straight to the school to see the Head. During that meeting she was given all the reasons why the school was concerned about our safety at home. They needed some answers about our life there before they could come to any conclusion as to whether to involve social services. Nan would need to find out what had happened over the last week in our home, otherwise they would have to take it further.

One compliment the Head paid Nan was about Sid. It was also a very large hint about how better it would be for Lucy and I to move in with our grandparents as well. Nan was told how our brother had performed exceptionally well in the yearly exams. Not only that, but all the teachers also saw the difference between him and us. He seemed both content and healthy ever since his address had changed from ours to Nan and Grandad's house.

By the time Nan left the school, her mind was made up, as was Grandad's after she had told him all about that meeting. He also agreed that she needed to find out as much as she could. Sid told me a little while later that Grandad had told him, 'Sid, please try and get honest answers from the girls.'

The first of two things that Nan had to find out about was the skin disease that I had developed. The Head had told her that it is often caused by a lack of hygiene and you can imagine how horrified my grandmother was. The Head also had said that, when another teacher had asked me about the medication I was getting for it, I said told her that Mum hadn't given me anything.

The other question she needed an answer to was how Lucy got that shocking bruising on her face.

After Nan had been to the school, she went round to see Mum and then returned and waited for us at the gates. She told us that she was picking up Sid and asked if we would like to come over and have some tea. Naturally, knowing that we wouldn't be seeing those awful visitors, we accepted her invitation happily. I think Lucy might have been a little puzzled that Nan didn't ask her what had happened to her face, or maybe she thought that she was being tactful in not mentioning it.

As far as Nan was concerned, those questions were to come later.

'I told your mother I was having you over for a while,' she said once we had arrived at her house. 'Thought you would like to spend a night here and then your grandfather will drive all three of you to school in the morning. I have a couple of pairs of pyjamas here for you.'

That was another invite we were happy to accept, as we would also get to spend time with Sid. What we didn't know was that our grandparents had no intention of letting us go back home.

During Nan's visit to Mum, she asked if she could help deal with the pile of dirty washing in the kitchen by putting on a load of towels and bedding, while she took as many of our clothes as she could home with her. Her reasoning was to ensure we had clean and ironed school clothes and some of our favourite things.

Sid must have been tasked with keeping me company so Nan could spend some time with Lucy. She needed some answers to a few questions but Lucy, ever loyal, still didn't tell Nan what was happening and stuck to the same story she had given to the teacher when she had asked with great concern about her black eyes and the large bruise on her face. Lucy maintained that she had tripped over one of her shoes and banged her head on her wardrobe door. The teacher had not believed that, neither had Nan. In her own way, Nan let Lucy know that it might have been a good story, but not a true one. The teacher told Nan that she believed it was caused by a fist, not a door – that was the main reason Nan had been asked to come to the school.

Lucy told me afterwards that Nan had looked at her sceptically and told her that the school believed that she was covering up for one of her parents.

'Georgia, I nearly did tell her the truth then, but I just couldn't bring myself to do it. I couldn't let Mum down.'

Luckily, Nan didn't ask me about it as I knew exactly what had happened, and I was not a good liar.

So, what did happen? We had been upstairs at home when Lucy told me about a game she had made up. Having read a few of the books she had found in our grandparents' house, there was a series of stories about a boy called William. Written in the 1920s, Lucy found them interesting as they showed that William led a somewhat naughty fictitious life at his boarding school.

'William never got caned, but he should have,' Lucy said, grinning at me. 'Now I'm going to be the new Head, I'm going to be a lot stricter. I have a list of questions that I will ask you, and if you don't get them right the first time, you will have to put your hands up for me to cane them.'

She managed to ask a few questions that I didn't have a clue about.

'Can't you ask me some easier ones?' I said.

'You don't talk to the Head like that! You're not a good pupil, now, are you? So, put those hands of yours out now.'

It wasn't a ruler she used, just a scarf that she flicked over my hands.

'Ooh!' I cried each time she 'hit' me.

Neither of us could believe what happened next. Mum flew into the room and yelled at Lucy. Before I could tell her that it was just a game, she had punched her in the face as hard as she could. The punch was so heavy, it nearly made Lucy fall over.

Without saying one word, Mum just turned around and walked out, leaving us both distressed and bewildered.

Straight away, Lucy's nose began bleeding profusely and her eyes were watering. She managed to ask me to go to the freezer and bring back one of the small bags of ice that were there. I went downstairs as quickly as I could and ignored Mum, who was sitting in her usual place on the sofa. She didn't even look up when I rushed into the kitchen to get that ice and the cleanest tea towel I could find.

Lucy was in tears when I got to our room and that was unusual as she rarely cried. She had put up with a lot, but never something like this. I wrapped the ice cubes in the towel so that she could hold them to her nose as she lay on the bed with her head back.

We spent the rest of the afternoon in our room. By the time we went downstairs for something to eat, all the ice cubes had melted but Lucy did say they had helped a lot. There was no sign of dinner being made and, although Mum had seen us, she said nothing. It was as if she had no memory of what she had done.

The rest of that day was a blank, although I can remember us getting up the next morning and going to school. By then, Lucy's face looked very sore and one of her eyes appeared to be bruised and her nose was swollen.

'I fell over,' Lucy said when we left for school. 'Just remember that, Georgia.'

'All right,' I said.

What else could we say?

I can still picture Sid coming over in our break and looking really concerned when he saw the bruises and swelling on Lucy's face.

'What on earth has happened to you, Lucy?'

She gave him the same answer that she told me she had already given to the teacher. 'I don't think she believed me,' Lucy had said when we met earlier.

She was right, she hadn't.

It was after the meeting with the Head that my grandparents finally came to a decision. They could put up with Mum damaging herself and letting the house fall into a state of disrepair, but they couldn't leave us all living under the same roof. They understood why we hadn't wanted to leave her, but now we had to accept that we no longer had a choice. Clare also agreed with her parents that Mum must go into rehab. If she refused again, then they would have to contact social services, who would take one look at the house and remove us. That was something that none of the family wanted to happen; they knew it would be distressing for all of us.

Nan felt that, as we were close to Clare, it would be better if she was the one to explain what was happening. She had agreed to this and decided to give us a nice surprise by turning up at the school gates. Lucy and I were delighted when we saw our aunt waiting for us. I noticed Clare blink when she saw the bruises on my sister's face, although she managed not to say anything. Instead, giving us a wide smile, she told us she hadn't seen us for a while, so she wanted to take us out for tea.

'Now, you two, jump into the car and I'll drive us to a really nice cafe I've found. You choose who sits in the front.'

'My turn,' said Lucy quickly, so I climbed in the back. After Clare had parked, we went into the cafe. With its large paintings on cream walls and comfortable padded chairs around light-oak tables, it was a little like the one Sid had taken us to, I thought.

Clare talked to us for a few minutes, then ordered scones with cream and jam, as well as cakes. While we were waiting for them, she said that she had to let us know what had been happening while we were at school. I had thought there might have been a reason why she had suddenly turned up to take us out, as of course, had Lucy. We exchanged glances and sat forward, sensing that what she was about to say was going to be significant.

'Your grandparents have gone over to talk to your mum' she said. Before she could say any more, Lucy butted in, 'What is it they want to talk about? Is that why we're here?' Before Clare could respond, Lucy continued to voice what was running through my mind: 'It's about us, isn't it?'

'Not really, although they're concerned about both of you. What I want to know, Lucy, is have you noticed that your mum's health is getting worse? Not only that, but your nan says the house is in a mess. It is, isn't it? Sid has finally told us about those people who were coming over, even before he left. He had hoped that had stopped, but it hasn't, has it? He described them to us, which was enough to make your grandparents really concerned. I don't think you meeting them when you get home is good for either of you, is it, Lucy?'

Lucy's shoulders sank and her head went down, defeated. 'No, I suppose not,' was her almost whispered response.

'And you, Georgia, what about you?'

'Some days I don't think she's the same mum,' I admitted.

From the expression that crept onto Clare's face, I realised that she, too, felt that her sister was a different person than the one she had grown up with.

'We all love her, you know, girls, which is why we want her to get better. Now, can you remember what it was like when your mum came back from hospital? She made you a promise then, didn't she?'

'Yes,' said Lucy sadly, 'I've not forgotten that – have you, Georgia?'

'No, I've not,' I said and I couldn't stop the words coming out. 'She told us she wouldn't take drugs any more.' Now that made Clare smile as I was so little to be talking about such things.

'She also said that Nan wanted her to go to a place where there were other addicts, but she didn't want to go,' Lucy added.

'And what do you two think about that idea now?' Clare asked.

'She should have gone, I suppose. She told us she could manage to give it all up on her own. I think she believed that she could. I know she tried hard, but she just wasn't able to.'

'I expect she did, Lucy, but now we've all seen her getting worse. I know there are days when she seems all right, but they don't last long, do they? I expect you two must have noticed it a lot more than we have, which is why we're all worried about you. We've come to a decision that it can't go on any longer.'

'No, I don't believe it can either,' said Lucy and she looked on the brink of bursting into tears.

Clare put a hand on her shoulder and squeezed it slightly. 'I know you've done everything you could, but now it's up to us adults to help both her and you. You and Georgia have done far too much already and have seen things no child should see. That's why Nan and Grandad are with your mother now. This time they won't accept any excuses about her not wanting to go to rehab, their feet are firmly on the ground now: your mum is to go to rehab, and that's it. They've already booked her in and Grandad's going to take her there tomorrow morning. Your nan will stay with her while she packs.

'Nan and Grandad aren't angry with her, but they want you to know that they feel guilty about not stepping in sooner. They have been aware of some of Paula's problems, but now they know there's a lot more. And Grandad's workmen have noticed how the house was being kept when they were sent to do some repairs.

'Won't you both feel relieved when she gets help? There's such a good chance that she'll come back feeling better. At least that's what we're all hoping for.'

'Clare, I want her to go too,' Lucy told her. 'She's not well and I haven't known what to do. But what will happen if she refuses, like she did before?'

'She's being told that, if she doesn't go, social services will arrive at her door and have both of you removed. I'm certain that would be enough for her to agree to spend some time in rehab. She really does love you, don't forget that.'

'Why would they do that?' Lucy asked.

Clare explained that the teacher who had seen my skin problem and then Lucy's bruised and swollen face had gone to the Head: 'Your grandmother is pretty convinced that if you continue staying in your home, social services would be called in. So, what did happen to your face, Lucy?'

To my surprise, Lucy managed to blurt out all the details of how Mum had come into our room and lashed out without saying one word. 'The worst thing, which upset me even more, was that she didn't seem to know what she had done. She didn't even ask if I was all right later on. That's when I felt she wasn't remembering things. I had noticed that for a while. It's as though some of what she had heard or said has been lifted right out of her mind, and that's not good, is it?'

'No, Lucy, it's not, which gives me another reason to want her to go. It's those drugs that make her do things like that – the sister I knew has changed,' Clare said sadly, before adding, 'Now, let's change the subject for a bit. Here comes the tea!'

We sat back as the waitress placed a pot of tea and the scones and cakes on our table. But any attempt to change the subject failed and, as soon as the waitress walked out of earshot, Lucy returned to it: 'What will happen to Mum in rehab?'

'She'll go to meetings with the other addicts, who will all tell their stories and why they want to be clean. And "clean" from a rehab point of view has nothing to do with washing, it means they have decided to stop taking drugs. Some people who left a while ago have written articles about their time in that rehab and how it changed their lives for the better.'

'Clare,' I said, 'if Mum doesn't go, would we be handed over to Dad? I know he's not living round here now, but he kept saying he wants us.'

'Why? Do you want to go to him?'

'No, I don't,' I told her.

'Just as well, as there's no chance of that, not after his shotgun antics and the restraining order. Anyhow, as it's your grandparents you will be staying with, the school will have no reason to contact social services. They know what a change it has made to Sid's results at school. So, there's nothing for you to worry about.'

It was then that Clare's phone rang. A smile came onto her face and then she answered: 'OK, Dad, I will.'

'Here's some good news for you both,' she told us. 'Your mum has agreed to go to rehab. She says she loves you both far too much for her to risk any problems with social services. Nan will go up the school and tell the Head that you're going to be staying with her and Grandad from now on. She'll be going back home afterwards, so once we've finished here, I'll take you both there. Your grandad is staying with your mum tonight as he's driving her to the clinic early in the morning.'

'Shouldn't we stop at our house and say goodbye to her?' I asked.

'And wish her lots of good luck?' added Lucy.

'No, not this time,' Clare said patiently. 'She's calm now

but seeing you two and knowing she has to leave you behind might upset her.'

What my aunt really meant was that Grandad didn't want anything happening that might change his daughter's mind about going. He wanted the rehab clinic to turn her back into the grounded, creative person who had written such beautiful short stories and composed all those emotive poems. He loved the daughter she had been, but he could barely recognise the one she had disappeared into.

31

Nan sent cleaners over to the house once Mum and Grandad had left. She also had them packing up all our clothes, books and bedding. Everything that could be washed, whether it was dirty or not, landed up in the washing machine. I could tell she was upset when she examined all those warts on my hands and on different parts of my body. How I hated them – they'd only recently appeared but I thought they made me look dirty and that was something I never wanted to be.

'Oh, Georgia, it's not dirt, it's just a little germ you've picked up. We'll soon sort them out,' she told me comfortingly. Nan never said that she blamed the state the house had been in, or that she had arranged to have the whole of it fumigated. She just told me that her doctor would prescribe something that would help my skin clear up.

The following afternoon she picked me up from school and took me there. Not that I can remember much about it as I was literally squirming with embarrassment. I know he looked at my hands and my body and told me that what he was going to prescribe would get rid of the warts. Thanks to Nan applying the thick liquid every day, they soon started to clear up.

It didn't take long for Lucy and I to feel totally at ease in our grandparents' large and comfy home. We no longer had to feel apprehensive about what we would face when we walked through the door. All we had to do was make our beds and put anything that needed washing into the wicker basket that Nan had placed in our room.

We soon realised that we were enjoying our new life. Getting our homework done was no longer a problem, we could just sit at the dining table and concentrate on it. We were also sleeping far more peacefully. It was Sid who observed that we were looking healthier: 'No dark rings under your eyes and both of you have nice pink cheeks now.'

We just giggled at this compliment, though in our heart of hearts we knew he was right. We were more energetic and finding our lessons at school much easier to concentrate on than we had before. It was so lovely to be with our brother again too.

When we were on our own, Lucy and I did talk about Mum. Naturally, we wanted her to be getting better and we wondered how she was doing in the clinic. Knowing that Nan was visiting her once a week, we kept asking her how our mother was getting on there.

Each time we asked, we were given the same answer: 'She seems to be doing quite well.'

Mum had been in that clinic for two whole months before Nan told us that she would be coming home soon:

'When we have the exact date, your Aunt Donna will come and stay here for a few days. She's asked me to tell you two that she's going to take you both out as she's not seen you for quite a while.'

I seem to remember that I was excited at being able to see Mum again, but I was also hoping that she would have changed back to the mother I was happy to be with. The one question that kept going through my head was, what would happen if she hadn't? I was a little shocked about Lucy not saying anything about Mum coming back. Her silence made me feel she was not as happy as I expected her to be.

'What's the matter, Lucy?' I asked when we were up in our room. 'Aren't you pleased we'll be seeing Mum soon?'

'I don't want to move back into the house straight away, Georgia,' she told me. 'Look what it was like after her hospital stay. I'm scared that the same things will happen again and I just couldn't cope with that. Don't think I'm being mean. Of course, I hope that Mum is cured now and doesn't want to touch any drugs, but I still want to wait until I'm certain she is. You see, what's on my mind is, if she really wanted to go and get herself cured for our sakes, then she wouldn't have had to be forced to go when she had no alternative, would she?'

'You mean Grandad forced her to go?'

'Not just him, she was forced by the school and Nan as well. That's why I've got a bad feeling that she won't be able to stay away from people like Bill for long.'

I didn't argue with my sister and only said that I was looking forward to seeing Mum. Though over the next few days, Lucy's words gradually turned over in my mind.

32

A week after we had been told that Mum would be returning, Aunt Donna arrived. Lucy had managed to repeat to Nan some of the reasons she had for not wanting to see our mother immediately.

'That's entirely up to you, Lucy,' she said calmly. I would now guess that she carefully omitted to say something else like 'who could blame you?'

One of the staff at the rehab, who had family living nearby, had offered to drive Mum home. 'Maybe a last-minute one-to-one,' Nan said. 'I'll be there at the house when she arrives, so I'll take some cooked meals with me. And your Aunt Donna and I will go out shopping later. I've already told your mum that I think it would be better if you two stay here a little longer – she needs to get settled in first. Of course, you can go over to see her any time when you're coming back from school. She was perfectly all right about that, though she did tell me she was looking forward to spending time with you both.

'I'll explain when I see her why you want to let her settle in for a bit, Lucy. How about you, Georgia, what do you want to do?'

'I'll go there after school,' I told Nan, although right from the beginning, something inside my head was telling me not to. It was as if words were coming into my mind and whispering, *don't, come back here instead*.

'I'll be spending quite a lot of time with your mum while you're at school,' Nan added. 'Your Aunt Donna is coming over as well. We've planned to go grocery shopping just before you arrive so you can have a chat on your own. I'm sure you have quite a few things that you want to tell her about.'

Actually, I didn't think there was much that I could say. I could hardly bring up how my skin was being treated, how I slept better and how safe I felt at Nan's. It was Mum's plans and how they would shape our future that I wanted to hear about.

During my lessons I had conflicting emotions. I was partly excited at the thought of seeing my mother again, but also nervous as well as I didn't know what she would be like after her treatment. As soon as school was over, I walked out of the gates as fast as I could. I missed not having Lucy walking along beside me. Once I got to the house, the habit of letting Mum know that I had arrived came naturally. I opened the door and called out the same simple words we always used: 'Mum, I'm here.' The moment she heard my voice, she was in the hall; her arms went around me and I was given hug after hug.

'Let's go in the living room,' she said and I smiled up at her. I could see the room looked slightly different. It had been painted again and was spotless without anything out of place.

There were fresh flowers on the table, which Nan must have brought her.

Mum sat down beside me, placed her hands on my shoulders and looked earnestly into my face: 'You're looking so good, Georgia, really healthy. Have you and Lucy enjoyed staying with your grandparents and Sid?'

'It's been nice there,' was about all I could manage. I could have told her some of the reasons I was happy there. Such as how I enjoyed the peace and quiet, as well as the cakes and meals that Nan cooked. Not only that, but Nan also ensured that all our clothes were clean and ironed, which made me feel much better at school. I didn't mention any of that, though, as I didn't want to hurt her feelings.

Instead, I just told her that she was looking great, which in a way she was. Her hair was back to being glossy, her skin looked a lot better and she had managed to put on a little weight since the last time I had seen her. But I wasn't sure if she was feeling as well as she looked. There was something in the expression in her eyes that for some reason made me feel apprehensive.

It was then that she leant a little closer to me and took hold of my hand. I can still remember nearly every word she said.

'I've been a terrible mother to you, Georgia.'

I could see tears beginning to swim in her eyes.

'No, Mum, you've not,' I managed to stutter.

'Thank you for lying, my darling, that's so sweet of you. I'm trying to let you know that you deserve much more than I've been able to give you. Over the time I was in that clinic I thought about you all a lot. As a result of all the therapy, I concluded that your lives would be much better if I wasn't here. I can see that Lucy wishes I hadn't come back home or else she would be with you, and as for Sid, he wants nothing to do with me, hasn't for a very long time. Not that I can blame him.'

I thought then that she must mean that she was planning to leave the area and go to another part of the country. Maybe to the town that was near the clinic she had been in for the last few months. Perhaps she had made friends with other women there? I really didn't want her to think that Lucy didn't care about her at all, so I tried to tell her that she was mistaken.

'She wouldn't want you to disappear, Mum. She wants Nan and me to tell her how you are and then she'll come over to visit you soon. And Mum, I want to keep seeing you but I won't be able to do that if you don't live here.'

But she only gave me a tight little smile in response before saying, 'Oh, darling, you're young, so it wouldn't take you that long to forget me.'

It was that remark that caused me to begin to feel uncomfortable. I had heard Mum talking nonsense when she was on drugs, but nothing like what she was coming out with now. I hoped Nan and Donna had finished their shopping so that they would be there very soon, although they had told me they wouldn't hurry as they wanted to give us some private time together. I just couldn't understand what Mum was trying to say.

If Lucy had been with me, she might have worked out what Mum was trying to tell me. Which was, of course, that her leaving this world would ultimately be better for her children in the long run. Though even if my sister had been there, it wouldn't have occurred to her that Mum had already put her plan in place.

I didn't know what to do – I just wanted her to stop repeating those words.

'Your life is going to be better without me,' she kept saying. Then she hugged me again before adding, 'It really will, darling.'

I wanted her to stop saying those things, so I told her I was thirsty. That made her get up and go over to the fridge to get me a cool drink. It was when she opened the door to the fridge that she collapsed onto the floor right in front of my eyes. For a moment I thought she had just slipped and would get up. She didn't. I walked over to her and kept saying the same words, 'Mum, Mum, get up please,' that I had used just two years earlier. It was when my knees gave way and I landed on the floor beside her that I could tell she was unconscious.

This can't be happening to us again, was all I could think. I told myself afterwards that I should have run out and got help from one of our neighbours. When I said that to my Aunt Donna, she told me that she could see that the shock of what I had seen had left me frozen, which meant I was incapable of moving. Luckily, Donna and Nan came through the front door with the shopping. I heard Nan gasp when she saw her daughter.

'Oh no, what's happened now?' she exclaimed as she dropped her bags of shopping on the floor and bent down to look at Mum.

When I recovered from my shock, I was told that it was Donna who had felt there was something wrong with her sister. Within a few minutes of leaving her in the house, she told Nan that she was convinced that they had to go back as soon as possible after picking up some groceries. It was also Donna who, placing her hands under my arms, had helped me get to my feet. She kept one arm round my shoulder and at the same time grabbed hold of Mum's handbag with her other hand. Once she got me sitting down on the sofa, she opened the bag and I saw her take out a small empty pill bottle.

'I thought so,' she said to Nan as she held it up. 'Looks like she's swallowed all the pills.'

'Oh no, Paula, darling,' I heard Nan say as she shook Mum's shoulder.

'Did she tell you anything, Georgia? Come on, think about what she said,' Donna asked and I found myself uttering those last words of Mum's. Out of the corner of my eye I watched as Nan moved over to the phone. That was the second time in my early childhood that I heard her voice explaining why we urgently needed an ambulance. Only this time there was a word – 'suicide' – which I didn't quite understand. Still, it sunk into my mind and stayed there.

When she had finished the call, Nan came over to Donna and me. 'Your mum will be all right, Georgia. She's just been a bit silly and taken too many pills by mistake.' She then asked Donna to take me back to her house. I can understand now why she didn't want me to see medics in the house again. My aunt still had her arm around me and my whole body was trembling as she led me to the front door.

'Try not to get upset,' Nan said. 'Your mum will be well looked after once she gets into the hospital. I'll ring Grandad when you're on your way and let him know I'm going to the hospital with her.'

I could tell that Donna was worried as well as angry with her sister. Holding my shaking body firmly, I heard her say to Nan, 'How could she do this in front of Georgia? Come on, Georgia, let's get you home.' As we walked out, I turned and looked at Mum lying unconscious on the kitchen floor.

That was the last memory I would have of her for a long time. Now, I can look back and understand more than a child of my age would have known. I might have noticed that there was a dazed look in her eyes. That might have told me that she had taken something. After all, Lucy and I were used to the signs. But perhaps I thought rehab had cured her so I was not looking for the telltale signals of drug use.

We never did find out where those pills had come from. What we do know was that, if Nan and Donna hadn't come back to the house so quickly, it's doubtful whether Mum would have lived. Yes, Lucy and I had saved her once, but this time I was too much in shock to do anything.

The doctor knew what type of pills they were after a tube had been put down her throat to suction them out. She had less than three hours left, was what he told Nan after she asked for an update.

Now, when I think about that day, I feel so sad that my mother was so broken that she wanted to die even while her youngest daughter was there with her. How terrible that she believed her leaving this world would have given me a better life. But although I hate to admit it, there was some truth in that.

33

Seven years later ...

It was when my school days were finished that I met Desmond, the man who took away the life I had and extracted every ounce of my confidence.

I remember Nan saying that I was no longer the same girl she had watched getting ready for the school prom just a couple of weeks earlier.

She was right, I wasn't.

Before I met him, I thought my teenage life was perfect. My final grades had been much higher than I had thought they would be, I had a group of good friends and, best of all, I had gained a place at Stanmore College in Harrow. I had wanted to study public health and social care for some time. My ambition was that I would eventually be able to help young and defenceless children, whose home life was far from good.

When Nan had seen the letter saying I had been accepted

at Stanmore, she said she was really proud of me: 'Not that many teenagers who apply to a college of further education have already decided what their future is going to be, but you have, Georgia.'

She told me later that she thought that she was just imagining a slight change in me. A couple of weeks on, she realised that her suspicions were real.

I can remember very clearly what happened during those weeks between writing the exams and going to Stanmore. My friends and I were all looking forward to celebrating the end of our school days. Half our conversation was about what we were going to wear and who we might choose to go with, and the other half was about future plans. We had been asked by boys in our year if we would like to be their partner but none of our group wanted to spend a whole evening with just one of them.

It was my closest friend Katie who said, 'If we really don't fancy going with any of the boys in our year, with their spotty faces and sweaty hands, I've an idea to put to you all.'

Don't get me wrong, it wasn't that we weren't friendly with quite a few of the boys in our year – after all, we had known most of them ever since we all started in the senior school. Liking them was one thing, fancying them was something else altogether. We all leant forward and asked Katie what her idea was.

'OK, here it is,' she announced as she flicked her thick dark hair back and grinned. 'We'll get dressed up in the most sparkly dresses we can find and all go together. Our point will be that we can go out without needing a male escort, and that way, no one who asked us to go with them will be offended. We'll just be a bunch of girls out to have fun.'

'Independent young women, you mean, don't you, Katie?'

'That's right. We'll be the new generation of successful young women, even if we are wearing long, feminine dresses. Oh, and hair and make-up that's got to look good. As for jewellery … well, we might have to raid our mums' jewellery boxes for that,' Katie added.

I had a pit in the bottom of my stomach hearing her say that.

But, despite it, we all went home in good spirits after our plotting.

I had a phone call later on that evening from my Aunt Donna. She told me that she was coming down to Nan and Grandad's as she hadn't seen me for a while. I told her about our plans for the prom and she laughed and said I'd better wear something that would make me stand out.

Donna wanted me to find the best shop for young people's evening clothes. That wasn't difficult as I already knew. Not that I had ever shopped there, but I had done a lot of window gazing.

I can remember how pleased I was that my aunt was visiting us. I was also hoping that Clare would be over soon too. But she hadn't long been married and was now pregnant with her first child so I would have to wait a little longer for that visit. Both my aunts had been so generous and kind to Lucy and me after that dreadful day when Mum overdosed. Donna had taken Lucy and me on some wonderful holidays in Cyprus, which she hoped would help make us forget the worst days of our childhoods. We loved it there. I can remember how Lucy had disappeared one evening and Donna and I went looking for her: there she was, crouching in the middle of a huge colony of stray cats.

Aunt Donna told her that we couldn't take them back to the UK and reassured her that they wouldn't starve. The number of animal-loving tourists who visited most of the year would ensure those strays were very well fed, she explained before adding, 'The restaurants and the residents also look after them, Lucy.'

On hearing this, my sister looked a little less worried, stroked the tabby who was rubbing itself against her and then came back to the hotel with us.

Happy days!

34

Ahead of Donna's visit, I did go into that shop to have a look. Every evening dress I saw there almost took my breath away, they were all just so beautiful. But I could hardly believe how much they cost. The shop assistant looked rather amused when she saw my face change as I glanced down at the price tags. She asked if she could help in any way and I told her that my aunt wanted me to find a shop that had suitable evening dresses for a prom night.

'I'm sure she will approve of our stock,' she said with a friendly smile.

I thought the same, but it was just their prices that bothered me.

After Aunt Donna arrived for lunch the following day, she asked me if I had taken a look at the shops. I told her I had seen some wonderful dresses, although the prices were very high.

'There's a big difference between an evening dress and a pair of jeans, Georgia,' she told me, stifling a laugh. 'Don't worry, we'll go there this afternoon and take a look.'

'You're right about this shop,' she reflected after we had viewed the magnificent window display. 'Very stylish. It's one of the best shops for your age group. I wish there'd been something like this when I was your age. Now, let's go in and have a closer look.'

The shop assistant recognised me straight away and gave us a welcomingly smile before asking my aunt if she could help. Donna told her exactly what it was we were looking for and three dresses were quickly pulled out. The price tag didn't stop my aunt encouraging me to try on the one that she thought might suit me most.

'It's up to you, though, Georgia,' she told me as the dress was whisked away to the changing room by the shop assistant.

With its tight-fitting bodice and ankle-length skirt in a floating pink silky fabric, I thought it was the most beautiful evening dress I had ever set my eyes on. There were metres of fabric in the skirt and I knew even without trying it on that this was the dress I wanted. As I came out of the changing room, there was the biggest smile on Donna's face I had ever seen.

'Oh my, you look really beautiful in that dress!' she exclaimed. 'Take a look at the tag and you'll see the style is named "princess" – and you certainly look like one in it. I think you love that dress, don't you?'

I did.

Within minutes, we had left the shop carrying an enormous posh carrier bag with my dress inside, wrapped in layers of tissue paper.

Being given that as a present because my exam results

had been good certainly gave me a great deal of pleasure. I had never worn anything like that dress before and I could hardly wait for the night of the prom. I felt so grateful that I couldn't thank my aunt enough. She just smiled.

Back home, Nan took one look at my dress and told both of us that she thought it was wonderful and her treat would be a pair of shoes to accompany it – 'I'm also going to lend you my pearls for your prom night, Georgia. They'll make you and the dress look even more lovely,' she told me. Silver high heels were my gift from Nan and they were perfect with the dress. Now, I only had to wait for two days before I would be wearing my outfit.

On the day of the prom I must have spent well over an hour getting ready. My hair had been blow-dried, my make-up carefully applied. Then it was time to put on the dress before stepping into the shoes. I gasped with delight when I finally put Nan's pearls round my neck. Knowing that she and Donna would want to spend a little time with me before I left, I went downstairs. I was right – they were sitting together, waiting to see me in my dress.

'You really do look like a princess!' Donna gasped.

'I think I can hear a car pulling up,' said Nan after she had made me walk up and down so that she could admire the dress even more.

I knew who the driver would be: Katie's dad. After hearing his daughter say that we wanted to go to the prom in a flashy limousine, he had told her that it would be a waste of money and, anyhow, who would notice us climbing out of it? At least his car was new and not an old banger. When Katie told us and asked if that was all right, we all agreed that this was a much better idea.

Once we got to the school, Katie's dad told us all to have a good time and said that he would pick us up later.

Soon, we were strolling into the seniors block, which had been decorated beautifully. The tall, good-looking DJ was already there when we walked in. He grinned at us each time he looked over in our direction. That night, he played great music which we could all dance to. It had a great rhythm that I'd not heard before, which encouraged us to dance with each other and the boys we had known for ages. Kylie's song, 'Can't Get You Out of My Head' was one that stuck in my head for days afterwards.

That night was truly amazing. It was full of laughter, music and dancing. I think every single person there had fun. There were plenty of soft drinks as well as food set out on the long tables – the teachers must have been pleased that not one bottle of alcohol had been smuggled in.

The balminess of summer was in the air and, with all the compliments that came my way, I began to feel like a princess in a fairy tale. I didn't know then that those were the last carefree days of my youth. If only flying carpets were real, then I could find one and tell it to take me back to those innocent and happy times.

35

Ever since I entered the final year of senior school, Nan's rules about having to be in by 9 p.m. were relaxed slightly, but she still wanted to know where I was going and who I was meeting up with. If it was a visit to family friends or relatives, she didn't mind me coming home a little later than that. She was also quite easy-going about me being out with the group of girls who she had come to know during my school years. In fact, ever since I came to live with her at the age of ten, she had really enjoyed having my friends over at the house. Nan had seen them becoming teenagers and there was not one she didn't admire.

About a week after the evening when I had gone to the prom, I mentioned that some of our group had invited me to join them at a pub. There was a weekly live music night. 'I love the sort of music they play there. There's a brilliant saxophonist coming, who's going to be playing on the night.'

'Yes, Georgia, I know those music nights are very popular. So, you go and have a good time and you can tell me all about it afterwards,' Nan told me. As she knew my group of friends hardly drank any alcohol, she wasn't worried about me spending the evening in a pub with them even though I was still underage.

That night when I got ready, I looked longingly at my prom dress, wondering, as I pulled on my jeans, if I would ever wear it again. *Well, at least not to where I'm going,* I told myself as I applied a small amount of make-up.

When I came downstairs, Nan said, 'You look just as lovely tonight, dear.' A photo of me in my prom dress was on the sideboard and she nodded towards it.

The evening was still light and warm and, looking up at the sky, I could see long streaks of deep pink edging it. The sight of it made me enjoy my walk to the pub. When I walked in, most of my friends were already there and had managed to bag the largest pine table, which was near the stage.

'Come on, Georgia,' said Declan, who was one of our group, 'there's a seat right next to me that you can have.'

'Thanks, be back in a minute then,' I told him as I went to the bar to get a soft drink before joining them.

A few minutes later, we all looked up as the musicians appeared and walked onto the stage, carrying their instruments. Just as they were about to begin, I noticed a good-looking man with very dark hair in his early twenties ordering his drink at the bar. He must have felt my eyes on him, for he turned around slightly and then gave me one of those smiles which makes a teenage girl go a little gooey.

That was the night I met Desmond. The one who changed my life, but not for the better. Not that I had a clue what was going to happen to me then. If only I had run back home, but then I was a very naive teenager in those days.

It was Declan who called him over and introduced Desmond to our group, although most of them seemed to have already met him before. There was a seat on the other side of me, which he pulled out and sat on.

'So, your name is Georgia,' he said. 'That's a name I've always liked.' Another of those smiles came my way. I began to feel my heart missing a beat, while a swarm of butterflies was fluttering in my stomach.

I couldn't get him out of my head when I went home that evening. I'd been tempted to stay longer, but decided to be sensible and so I left in plenty of time to get home by ten. I was pretty certain that Nan would still be awake and listening for the click of the front door, even though her light was off.

Once I was in my room, Desmond's smiling face with those dark-blue eyes kept sliding into my mind. I must have spent half the night tossing and turning, wondering how I was going to meet him again.

But I needn't have worried. Declan had also been invited to my cousin's birthday party. As he was friendly with Desmond, he brought him along. When I saw the pair of them in the living room, I could hardly believe it, and just a few minutes' later, Desmond came over, carrying his glass of wine and one for me.

'Nice to see you again, Georgia. Declan told me you liked wine so I thought I would bring one over to you.'

'I do, thanks,' I said, just about glowing with pleasure.

Soon we were chatting away and, when I glanced over his shoulder, I could see Declan grinning at us.

'Thought you two would get on,' he said smiling when he came over to us, but then he noticed a couple coming in who he also knew. I think both of us were quite pleased when he wandered off, leaving us alone again.

Both Desmond and I said we thought this was a good party. Soft jazz was being played, bottles of wine were being opened, while large platters of food were passed around. I told myself not to drink more than one more glass of wine. Thankfully, my cousin's friends were not big drinkers so there were plenty of soft drinks on offer. On occasions like this one I inevitably knew most of the people there. 'I'd better go and say hello,' I told Desmond, but he just smiled and said, 'Off you go then, I'll catch you later.' He did too. After about half an hour he was by my side again – 'Shall we get some food and sit down for a while? There are a few chairs in the conservatory that no one is using.'

I followed him over to the dining table and helped myself to a plate of food before making my way to the conservatory. There, I perched on one of the chairs – ones that we hardly left for the rest of the evening. I felt like we were really getting to know each other but what I would come to realise later was that, although he had got to know me fairly well, I hadn't seen the real Desmond at all. I was much too busy feeling flattered by his attentions than to see anything but his charm.

He appeared interested in every word that came from my mouth. When he asked about my exams, I told him all about the course I was going to be joining in just a few weeks at

Stanmore College. That made him pat my hand and say, 'Good for you, Georgia – I'm really impressed by your ambition.'

He then told me about his wealthy father, who lived in Ireland. 'He's an actor,' he said to my surprise. 'A very well-known one. Not that I keep telling people that, but he's been in a lot of films.' He mentioned some of them, including one that had been released about a year earlier.

'I saw that one!' I told him excitedly before adding, 'I think you must take after him a bit as far as features go. Maybe that's why I was looking at you the other night.'

He laughed at that.

'I might look like him, but we're very different people. He gives me an allowance, though.'

'So, you're Irish then?'

With his black hair and dark-blue eyes, he certainly looked like he could be.

'Yes, but I don't feel that way. Anyway, I prefer living in London. This city feels like home to me – there's not enough for me to do over there.'

Desmond must have guessed that I wanted to know more about him, such as the type of career he was aiming for. He then asked me some more about the course I would be taking after the summer holidays and what I had decided to do afterwards. I told him some of the reasons I wanted to be a social worker in a few years.

'I have dreams of what I might be working at in the future,' he told me, 'but in the meantime, I'm with a removal company.'

I didn't ask too many questions about his work as it sounded pretty boring.

During that evening Desmond asked me if I would like to go with him to his favourite wine bar in a few days' time. 'Do you know it already?' he asked after telling me the road it was on.

'Funnily enough, I've had been there with my friends a few times, and yes, I really like it there,' I told him.

'It always has good music and the atmosphere's great, isn't it?'

'It's a fun place,' I agreed.

Of course, I'd been hoping that he would want to see me again and I couldn't stop myself from smiling away until he mentioned that he would pick me up at eight. I had to tell him then that it was a bit late – unless I was at a relative's house, I was expected to come home between nine and ten. I also mentioned the fact that my grandparents always wanted to know who I was meeting up with. 'But I'll just tell them I'm going out with a few of my friends,' I told him.

He looked quite amused by that, especially when I asked him to meet at the end of our road and said not to come to the house. I was pretty sure that my grandparents would not be pleased about me going out with someone they hadn't met. I felt pretty unsophisticated bringing that up, but he seemed to understand and agreed to pick me up at six thirty instead.

What I didn't know was that Desmond already knew a lot about me.

* * *

When I left the house, he had parked his expensive-looking car at the end of our road. Looking back, I remember it took me quite a long time to realise that the removals he carried out were not with the owner's consent. His small company frequently removed goods from homes, garages and even whisked some things straight out of the delivery trucks being unloaded on the streets.

My other memory of our early dates was how he tried to persuade me to think that Nan's way of looking after me was wrong. That made me feel very confused. It was the beginning of my happy life changing forever.

36

During my early teenage years, I accepted Nan's curfew times without question. It was not until I met two people who gave me other ideas that my opinions gradually started to alter. I was also aware, almost as soon as I met them, that these people would not be welcome in my grandparents' house. Not only that, but if Nan knew that I was meeting up with them, she would be pretty angry. And that was something I didn't want to happen.

Over the years since I had moved to Nan and Grandad's, I had become used to them wanting to know who I was mixing with. Now, as a mother myself, I can see that they wanted to keep an eye on Lucy and I in case we had inherited some of our mother's weakness or, even worse, our father's complete inability to tell the truth. It was after I met Desmond that I began to resent what I was beginning to see as undue interference.

Those were the thoughts slowly placed in my head, but not just by one person, but two. The first one was Desmond, who having asked me out, quickly became important to me. Even then, I knew instinctively that I should not bring him home. I had no doubt that Nan would not approve of him. She would be able to tell straight away that he had little ambition and him saying that he had dreams for his future would hardly impress her. When I went out on dates with him, I was able to make her believe that I was going out with my girlfriends, who she knew.

I understand now why Nan wanted me to do well at college as she saw that as the beginning of my future career. She certainly didn't want me going the same way as Lucy, who had not bothered about her exams and was now living with her boyfriend. That event had certainly caused ructions and hugely disappointed Nan. I had a pretty shrewd idea that, after Lucy gave up on her education, the last thing Nan wanted was for me getting tied up with a young man, especially one who hadn't tried to go to university or taken a job which could lead to a successful career.

The second person was my father. Nan would have been, if not furious, then hurt about me meeting up with him again. He was the one person who my grandparents never wanted to come anywhere near our family. Sid, who was still living at home with Nan and Grandad, would have agreed with them wholeheartedly. To his mind and that of our grandparents, our father had broken the law. Not only that, but most people would view him and his delinquent brother Simon as dangerous characters. None of us had forgotten how they had treated Mum or the time they threatened her and then my grandparents with a shotgun. Again, in hindsight,

I can now agree that I made a bad mistake in letting Dad back into my life.

Just two days after I had been out with Desmond, much to my surprise, I was to see my father again. It was actually Lucy who was meeting him and I found myself begging to see him with her. At first, she refused, but she soon gave in. Of course, I had mixed feelings about seeing him after everything that had happened. What I found hard to work out was why Dad was back in town.

I only told Nan that I was meeting up with my sister and made no mention that I might see Dad. She might have disapproved of Lucy's lifestyle, but she would never try to stop our friendship. After all, Lucy was the sister who had looked after me when we were both much younger.

'Do you know why he's here?' I asked Lucy when we met.

'I don't really know, Georgia,' she told me. 'I think he just wanted to meet up with his children again, but Sid said a flat no.'

'How did he find you then? You moved out of Nan's quite a long time ago and you haven't had your mobile for long.'

'I've sort of been keeping in touch occasionally and I gave him my new address,' she told me hesitantly.

'Why didn't you tell me?'

'Because he had upset you too much. I wanted to wait and see if you ever talked about him, but you only did once. That was a few years back, when you blamed him for the night Mum tried to kill herself. But you must know now that was not the real reason she did what she did, don't you?'

'Maybe not, but I did know that Mum was terrified of

him. It wasn't until the police told her he had vanished from the area that she felt safer. I remember how relieved I was when Mum told me that he had definitely gone. But as long as you're there, I'll come.'

We started to walk to the pub where Lucy was meeting him, but she kept glancing at me and I realised I was walking very slowly.

'You won't change your mind about coming with me, will you, Georgia?'

'No, I said I would,' I told her firmly. 'I've managed to put a lot of my past behind me. As well as the frightening things he did, I can't help remembering a few of the nice times with him. I did love him when I was small and I suppose I'm curious about what he's like now.'

As the pair of us went into the bar, I just about choked with the thickness of the cigarette smoke in the air.

'Couldn't you have found another place to meet him?' I asked. Looking around, it seemed nearly everyone in that crowded bar was holding a cigarette up to their lips.

'I'll try next time – all this smoke makes it stink in here, doesn't it?' she agreed.

This was the kind of pub I would never normally go into, but I should have known that it would be the sort of place Dad would have chosen. Even though he had changed quite a lot since I last saw him, I recognised him almost straight away but I noticed that he looked a lot older than I expected. His hair was thinner and greyer, his once-fit body no longer lean and muscular. He was leaning on the bar with a drink in his hand and it only took a glance to tell that he was already drunk, but at least now it neither surprised nor frightened me.

Just as I was about to say hello, I felt his gaze fix on both of us, but it was only Lucy he spoke to: 'Good of you to come, darling. I see you're not alone. Now who's that you have with you?' He pointed his nicotine-stained finger at me and it shook in the air. 'Is she a mate of yours?'

Lucy just about fell over laughing at this and I said indignantly, 'Yuck, Dad, do you honestly not recognise me? I'm your other daughter.'

From the look of amazement on his face I could tell that the memory of me he had kept in his head was when he had last seen me. I had only been ten then and over the years since he couldn't have pictured me growing up.

'Georgia, is that really you? I never thought I'd see you again.'

As he moved closer to me, I nearly pulled myself away as the stench of tobacco and alcohol on his breath assaulted my nose. Instead, as I had a feeling that maybe he had missed me a lot, I managed to smile at him and say, 'Yes, it's me, Dad.' If I wasn't the daughter who had stayed in his memory, neither was he the father in mine. I had expected to meet the strong, powerful man he had once been, not someone who looked old and weak.

On the way there I had reminded Lucy that I must be back in the house by nine – 'Nan knows I'm meeting up with you, but I don't want any questions asked, like where we went.'

'Poor you!' Lucy said with a grin. Still, she looked at her watch when I did at around eight thirty and told Dad we had to go.

'I'll give you a call later on this week,' Lucy told him and, standing up on her toes, she gave him a kiss on the cheek.

In the back of my mind all I could think about was how the smell of the smoke on my clothes and hair would give me away to Nan and, as we walked into the fresh air, I took deep breaths and tried to get as much air as I could into my hair and clothes.

As she walked back with me, Lucy and I discussed Dad. It wasn't just that he looked so much older, it was the number of drinks we had seen vanishing down his throat.

'There's no mistaking that he's gone from being a bit of a heavy drinker to being an alcoholic,' I said, but Lucy just shrugged.

Stay away from him, he's going to cause trouble again, my inner voice told me, but I felt too sorry for Dad to do that. I knew that if I didn't arrange to see him again, he would be terribly upset.

To begin with, I went with Lucy to meet him and then I went on my own. I persuaded him to come to my favourite wine bar, the one I had been to with Desmond. The seats were comfortable and I loved the cocktail menu, which also included a long list of mocktails.

'What are they? Fizzy drinks without alcohol?' Dad looked puzzled when I ordered one.

I told him that I didn't drink much and there was no way that I could go home looking as though I had.

'All right, I'll stick to wine then. Just a couple of glasses, if that makes you happy,' he told me.

It did, especially as he ordered some food for us and stayed sober for the rest of the evening. That made it much easier for me to be out with him. He asked me what my plans were and I told him about going to college, which seemed to impress him. It was then I made a mistake, not that I realised it then.

I told him all about Desmond.

37

As I had met up with Dad, I started thinking about a visit to Mum. I might as well have both my parents in my life, for better or for worse – after all, they were still my parents.

Nan had told me that Mum now lived in a flat within walking distance of our home. It was just that my last memory of her made me hesitate. Lucy had told me a few things about her too. Several years ago, Mum had met a man who she was fond of and they were still together. The next thing Lucy told me was that she hadn't completely stopped taking drugs, but she had managed to give up most of them.

When I plucked up the courage to tell Nan that I wanted to go and see Mum, Nan looked very pleased and wrote the address and Mum's phone number down for me. She did tell me that both she and my mother had understood why it had taken me so long to want contact with her. I knew Lucy had visited her often, but Sid, like me, had stayed away.

'I don't know if Paula ever thought you would want to see

her again,' Nan said. 'She's been hoping that you would be able to forgive her one day.'

'I've tried to push away that memory and all the emotions they cause, Nan. But I think I'm all right about it now,' I told her.

I asked Nan to make the call and tell Mum I was coming over.

When I knocked on the door, Mum opened it so quickly that I suspected she must have been standing right next to it. I had to stop myself from looking shocked at the change in her appearance. It was a good thing that Nan had warned me that she had aged a lot; it wasn't only that she looked nearly ten years older, it was that her beautiful looks, with the exception of those huge blue eyes, had almost faded.

The first visit was easier than I thought it would be. Nan telling her to expect a young woman rather than a child must have prepared her and she looked really happy to see me when I arrived at her door.

'Come in, Georgia,' she said as she opened the door wide and took me into her small living room. I glanced around and saw she was reading a book, which was the only thing lying around. The room was spotless and, with all the cushions and pictures on the walls, it looked really cosy. She didn't ask about why I hadn't wanted to visit her for so long, but I could tell how happy she was by my arrival and she told me I looked so grown up and beautiful.

After telling me to sit down, she went to get us some tea and biscuits – she must have had everything ready as she was back almost immediately. She told me about Nan bringing over some family photos and letting her know how well I was doing at school.

'So, at least I did see you growing up that way,' she said and I could see that this had saddened her.

Soon, I found chatting to her easy. I listened to her telling me about her partner, who she had been with for several years. From what she said, he really cared for her and there were no arguments or bullying in her home. This I could tell had made her feel content and cared for. Naturally, she, in turn, then asked me questions about my friends and asked if I had a boyfriend.

I managed to tell her quite a lot about the friends I had known for several years but avoided mentioning Desmond and our dates altogether. That would have been unfair as I would then have to ask her not to tell Nan.

As Lucy had said, Mum appeared to have cut down on her drugs, but had not given them up entirely. There were some occasions when we met up when I realised she was on something, but she was never out of it in my company and I decided not to criticise her and neither did Nan any more. I just accepted her as she was and enjoyed spending some time with the person she now was.

38

It was after my first date with Desmond that I became convinced we were now in a relationship that would soon become a serious one. I found my mind was filled with those thoughts for much of my day. Over the years I wished I had known about the problems that both my grandparents were facing at that time. If I had, I would have understood that Nan's lack of sleep was not because she wanted to know what time I came in, but concern about her husband's gradual decline.

She has been someone who seldom shared her problems. If only for once she had confided in me, I might have been mature enough to change what I was getting up to behind her back. Or to put it a better way, surely my younger self would have acted in a less selfish way and put my grandmother first.

To be fair, I didn't know much about dementia then. All I noticed was that Grandad was rather forgetful and not his usual self, which I put down to him being nearly 80. Nan, on the other hand, was totally aware that over the next few years he would get a lot worse.

When Nan and Grandad decided to let his company go, I didn't question it. I just assumed that Grandad had already retired, as most of his workmen were also reaching retirement age. All Sid said about the company being closed was that Grandad no longer wanted to do any paperwork. He didn't tell me the real reason, which was that Grandad could no longer add up or understand why prices had gone up on goods that had to be delivered, meaning they often lost money when carrying out quoted work.

Sid thought that it was up to Nan to explain the situation to her grandchildren and, if she didn't wish to tell me, then he wouldn't either. I can remember quite clearly my brother telling me around then about his future career plans. I was pretty amazed that he was joining the police force.

'Is Mum the reason you have joined the force?'

'Partly,' he told me. 'I have to say thank goodness you have never been tempted to take drugs, Georgia. I think we all hated those people we met when we were younger too.'

'I saw the damage it did too and, remember, I was only eight at the time and I should never have been made to see everything that was going on. Do you know that, even if I have a headache, I still feel scared of swallowing an aspirin in case I get addicted to over-the-counter drugs? But it's the bigger dealers I loathe. Hope you and your colleagues catch those rich bastards!' I said.

Sid gave me a brotherly hug and told me he was pleased to

see how I had grown up: 'No weakness in that direction then and, from what I've heard, you hardly drink either.'

Now, that was true then. My fear of drugs, even prescribed ones, has remained with me right up to today. However, being a mild drinker was something that would change.

Sid was not someone who repeated conversations or gossiped about other people. For example, he never told me that Clare had explained exactly what had caused our mother to be rushed into hospital for the second time. Years later, when my aunt told me herself, she said she couldn't tell how he felt about it. Even as a young boy, Sid was always able to keep his feelings tucked well away.

Not only had Sid been given the details of the day Mum nearly died, but Lucy had too. She felt really bad that she hadn't gone with me to Mum's that day, acknowledging that being on my own then must have been very traumatic. A short while after that incident, Lucy, who still loved our mother, began visiting her secretly, although I was unaware of that for a long time.

Lucy had agreed with Mum that I should wait until I was old enough to decide if I wanted her back in my life.

39

My lack of knowledge about what was happening in my grandparents' lives meant that I listened to Desmond every time he came up with what he thought was a good idea. That gave him the opportunity to put thoughts in my head. Especially on the matter of how late I should be allowed to stay out: 'You're not a schoolgirl now. It's college you're going to and students can come and go as they please. Do all your friends have to get permission to leave the house? I don't think so!'

I couldn't disagree with that. Maybe he had got it right, maybe he hadn't, but by then I was falling in love and clinging onto almost every word he said.

It was after we had been to the wine bar a couple of times that he told me he wanted to take me to a really special Italian restaurant – 'Not one that serves dishes of spaghetti but real Italian food. I think you'll enjoy it, it's quite sophisticated.'

Of course, every young girl on the cusp of womanhood wants to feel special and sophisticated, and he was right about the restaurant – I thought the food was great and the atmosphere in the beautifully decorated dining room was wonderful.

That night I managed to get home just a few minutes before 11. Nan didn't seem happy when I walked in, which I assumed must be because I was a little bit late. In fact, she was worried about Grandad, which was why she was making him a chamomile tea to help him get to sleep.

Again, it didn't enter my head that I was not the reason she was up. I told her that a friend had taken me out for a meal and that it had taken a bit longer to finish than I expected.

'You could have rung me,' Nan said as she picked up the tea and headed upstairs, which added to me thinking she disapproved of my being a little late.

The following morning, when I came down into the kitchen for breakfast, Nan seemed rather quiet. She didn't mention anything about my being out late. Nor did she ask me where I had been, which made me think that she had other thoughts in her head.

Thank goodness, my inner voice said, *no questions*. Again, I had no idea that it was Grandad she was concerned about. He had another appointment at the surgery so that his GP could assess how far his dementia had progressed. That must have been what she was thinking about that morning. I, on the other hand, was wondering what excuses I could come up with for my next date with Desmond. I couldn't use Lucy's name again – seeing her so often might just give Nan a shrewd idea that it was not always my sister that I was spending time with. Occasionally, I had told my grandparents casually that I was going out to meet up with some friends and, without any further explanation, I had left. It was about then that Nan, who had all those other worries on her mind, must have just hoped she didn't have a reason to be suspicious about my evenings out.

In the end, strongly influenced by Desmond, I found myself believing I had to leave home, the one I had lived in for seven years. I was completely aware that I had managed to make my grandmother both disappointed in me as well as being more than annoyed. I should have faced up to the fact that it was all my fault and apologised. But then teenagers seem to have a knack of refusing to take the blame. I'm sure, as you read this, you might be nodding as you remember your own late teens.

Now I can explain it all a lot better than my teenage self would have. I had been out with Desmond, who had booked us into the same restaurant again. As before, cocktails immediately came my way, followed by wine, which was generously poured throughout the meal.

Desmond brought up the subject of music when we finally ordered some cheese and biscuits rather than dessert: 'I know you love live music, Georgia, and there's a really good band playing not far from here. Shall we go?'

I remember looking at my watch and telling him I couldn't go for long as I had to be in at a decent time. Naturally, he raised his eyebrows at that.

'Oh, come on, Georgia, be real! You're not a child now, so don't act like one. Grown-up girls do what they want to. So, are you coming with me or not?'

I could tell he wasn't joking and so I quickly told him that, of course, I was.

He was right about the music: it was good and, as we listened to it, I hardly dared look at my watch. Desmond kept his arm round my shoulder for most of the evening and made no movement to leave until a few minutes before the club closed, which was not far off 2 a.m. I must have prayed that everyone would be asleep when he dropped me off and I snuck in, taking off my shoes at the front door and closing it as quietly as I could before creeping slowly up the stairs to my room. I should have known that Nan would want to know exactly what time I had come in. In the morning, I wondered if she had even closed her eyes before she heard me arriving, but even if she hadn't, she would ask.

If coming in late was to cause me a problem, Nan, knowing all the neighbours nearby, was to cause me an even greater one. It hadn't occurred to me that I might well have been seen being picked up by a young man in a fairly new car. What I didn't know was that Nan had already been told about that but had decided to wait a while to see if I would tell her who he was.

If she had told me about being seen getting in the car with Desmond the day that she had heard about it, I might have been able to find some excuse. Unfortunately for me, it was the night I was out so late that she also heard about me meeting up with Dad more than once, which for her was extremely upsetting and showed a lack of loyalty. I suspect it might have been one of the men who had been part of Grandad's team, who often visited, who tipped Nan off. One phone call was all it took, I was told. Those workmen would have clearly remembered the shotgun business as well as Dad and his brother attacking Mum in her own home. Even though they had worked with Dad, they were aware of his lawless actions, including pinching the money that Grandad had invested in the house.

Hearing about me getting into his flashy car annoyed Nan, but not mentioning that Dad was back was even worse. Knowing that I was out with him and looked as though I had been enjoying myself not only hurt her feelings, but also infuriated her.

The moment I came downstairs, Nan told me to sit down as she had a couple of things that she wanted to talk to me about. I thought this must be about the time I got in late; perhaps she wanted to know just what I'd been up to. Although I was nervous, I still thought I could just tell her about the music and that I was so enjoying it, I hadn't realised how late it was.

I was wrong.

'You never said a word about your dad being around here,' was her opening sentence. 'Now, can you explain why that is? And don't try telling me you only bumped into him when you were out with your sister.'

I tried to say he looked older and weaker and that now there was nothing frightening about him, 'and I just felt sorry for him.'

'Sorry for a man who beat up his wife and stole from us and then threatened us with a shotgun?' She was really angry now. 'So, anything else that's made you pity him?'

My cheeks were flaming as there was nothing I could say then.

'I'm surprised you can't think of at least one of your excuses, Georgia, seeing as you keep telling me that you're going out with your sister. Funny that she sends a man in a shiny dark-blue car who picks you up at the end of the road. And now you're coming in really late without having told me the name of the person you're seeing, nor where you've been until well after midnight.'

I was now not only red, but also close to tears.

'If that's disappointing behaviour, not telling me the truth about where you were going and who with is even worse, especially if it isn't your sister. And if that's disappointing, meeting your father is even worse. He's lucky he didn't end up in prison – he deserved to be more than once, I can tell you. Surely, you've not forgotten that day when your mum was dragged out of the house half-naked in front of all the neighbours?'

I tried to give her an answer, but she was in full flow now.

'Shush, Georgia, I don't want to hear anything now. I don't understand why you've lied and lied to me. You need to think now, not talk. All I'm saying is that, if you keep on doing this, you'd better find somewhere else to live. Maybe move in with your sister since you've been telling me how you spend so much time with her. And by the way, I don't want your mother to know that you've been seeing your father. Have you forgotten how frightened of him she's been?'

I was desperately fighting to stop the tears from coming then. Nan had never been so angry with me before and, deep down, I knew it was all my fault. She told me then that she needed to go out and got off her chair quickly. Without another word, she left the room.

I sat there wondering what I could do. Let's just say what I decided then was another of my big mistakes.

After the row with Nan, I stood frozen to the spot until I heard the sound of the front door closing firmly behind her. My grandmother had told me that she needed to do some shopping and was then going to see Mum, but she didn't invite me. Foolishly, I felt that I was being excluded from my family and it made me feel even more fragile.

A long time ago, my adult self finally realised that Nan just needed some time to think about how she could sort out our relationship. She wanted it to work, but she didn't want to give in to me either. That was the main reason she wanted to see Mum as she was now the only daughter who lived nearby and she would understand more about what I'd been getting up to.

I learnt from Mum about a year later that she had pointed out that times had changed since Nan had been my age: 'You were born in the early forties, Mum. Times have changed – young women are freer and more independent now than when you were Georgia's age. You didn't meet Dad in a bar, did you?' And they both laughed. Mum already knew that her parents had met in the home of a family friend. Back then, girls just didn't walk into bars on their own. Mostly they met their future husbands through people their parents knew.

Mum told me that her words made Nan reflect on her memories of what life for girls was like back in the late fifties. She admitted that, when they reached the age of wanting to meet a suitable partner, girls would have to get their parents' approval before they could walk out of the house to meet a boy.

Being independent then would have been nigh on impossible. Two generations before I was a teenager, men still earned a higher hourly rate than women doing the same job. Not only that, but women also had to get their husband's or father's written permission to open a bank account of their own. Goodness knows how women who were single or widows managed to keep their families going. At 17, my friends and I had learnt quite a lot about how, after the First World War, women fought for the right to vote. We felt that it was partly due to them that our lives were so much better than our predecessors.

There were other things that Nan talked about with Mum that day. I wish I had known the saddest thing they discussed: my grandfather's descent into dementia. It was, in fact, that and not my behaviour that was causing her so much stress. Mum told Nan that one of the things she remembered from rehab was that an excess of anxiety can stop people thinking logically. On hearing this, Nan thought about her last conversation with me and then she realised that she had been a bit harsh.

Now, remember, I had no knowledge of her worries. Instead, I was thinking that she must have gone out because she was so disgusted by my behaviour and didn't want to set eyes on me again for a while. And Grandad didn't seem in the least bit bothered by what I'd been up to. When I went in to use the phone, he was sat in his chair in the living room looking half-asleep. He managed to open his eyes a little wider before he gave me one of his friendly smiles.

I didn't think to question his behaviour at the time.

Clare had given me a mobile phone for my birthday so I could hardly use the one in the living room. I made an excuse to Grandad and went upstairs to my room to phone Desmond. Looking back at that day, I would say that my younger self should have done several things differently before she blurted everything out to someone she hardly knew.

First of all, the most sensible move would have been to wait for Nan to get home and then offer her a sincere apology. After all, wasn't she the person who had looked after me for all those years? So, where was my gratitude? I am now ashamed of how I handled it.

Second, if I didn't have the courage to wait for Nan, then wouldn't it have been a good idea to phone my sister? Lucy would have invited me over and let me stay with her until everything calmed down. She wouldn't have agreed with my assumption that Nan wanted me out of the house and would have explained to me that I had just annoyed her. Besides, Nan hadn't thrown a suitcase in my room and told me to start packing! I would say that this burst of temper was soon regretted and I can hardly blame her for it. As for me?

My walking out was just a piece of obstinate teenage behaviour, wasn't it?

As soon as I was on the phone to Desmond, I couldn't stop myself blurting out all the details of the row I had had with Nan.

'That sounds dreadful, Georgia,' he told me. 'How long is your grandmother likely to be out?'

'At least a couple of hours, I think. She's going to see Mum after she's done her shopping.'

'You'd better get out of that place. You can stay with me a long as you want to. Best thing you can do is cram as many clothes as you can in a suitcase and I'll come and pick you up in an hour. Stop worrying, I'll have you out of that house in no time at all.'

By the tone of his voice, I could tell he was really pleased that I would go to where he lived and be with him. I felt a warm feeling of being wanted and knew that he must be very fond of me to want me to live with him. Just the thought made me feel excited and cheered me up no end. What Desmond really felt, I realised a few months later, was that getting me to leave home was a personal triumph. He must have raised his fist and done an air punch and shouted out with joy when he heard that his plan of keeping me out late had worked just the way he wanted it to.

I wish now that I hadn't told him about my grandmother nearly always being awake when I came in. And as I've said, I had also mentioned that she was rather strict about the time she felt I should be home by. He must have known that coming back several hours after the expected time would likely cause a huge row. Certainly, getting me to sip away at more alcoholic cocktails than I had ever had meant that I didn't notice how time was flying.

There's always a pivotal moment that can wreck our future, isn't there? Not that we plan it that way, but young love can make us blind to reality, and if only we were more mature, we might be more discerning. I didn't recognise that I was about to walk into a darkness which would prevent me from seeing the evil that was lurking for me in the shadows.

Up in my bedroom, I pulled down clothes from my wardrobe and tossed them in my suitcase, which was full in minutes. I managed to find a couple of carrier bags to sling in underwear and make-up. What was I thinking? I could admonish my younger self now and say that to her. How could I have written that note to Nan saying I was leaving as she didn't want me in her home any more. No decent explanation as to why I was leaving, no words of thanks for all that had been done for me. All I could think was that I would ask Nan to send on the rest of my things once I had an address.

Desmond didn't hang about. He rang once he was in our road and, picking up my luggage, I went out without saying a word to Grandad. My boyfriend got out of the car, opened the boot and quickly put my luggage in.

'In you get,' he said, giving me a quick hug before I climbed in.

Now, I would ask just how stupid I could have been to climb into Desmond's car and let him take me to a place I knew nothing about. But then I thought I knew him, but I clearly didn't, did I?

I can remember so well that journey in the car, where I could see him smiling broadly. When we were at traffic lights, his hand would squeeze my knee and he kept saying, 'Bloody lights, holding us up.' Once they changed, he drove pretty fast, as he usually did. His driving didn't make me nervous as Dad's had done, so for all his faults, I can say he was a pretty good driver. All the time I sat in the car I wondered what his place was going to be like. After all, his father was rich, and hadn't Desmond said that he gave him an allowance? It was those statements that gave me the impression of a large, well-furnished and comfortable flat. But when he pulled up and said, 'Here we are,' I was disappointed. The building he was pointing to was some kind of hostel – hardly luxurious.

'That's where I'm staying at the moment,' he told me. 'Got a nice room, which we can share. Plenty of room in my wardrobe for you to hang your clothes up.'

I hadn't expected anything like this. I had imagined a lovely two-bedroom place where I would cook good meals and, as we got to know each other more, our relationship would blossom. I can't remember much about the place I walked into with him, just that I felt uneasy about it being a room, not a flat. Memories of all those slummy places we had lived in with Mum flooded back. Also, I hadn't told him that I was a virgin, which made me nervous. There were certain things he said that made it clear that he expected us to share a bed. That was far from what I had expected. Silly me, I should have asked him if he had a spare bedroom when I phoned. If he hadn't, I could have gone to my sister's but now it was too late. Up until then it was only kissing and cuddling and I still felt that it was too soon to go any further.

When Desmond opened the door to his room and I walked inside, all I saw was a double bed, a couple of chairs, a small table and a television. It was enough to almost make me burst into tears. I was already upset by the way I had left Nan's. Deep down, I knew that I had made a terrible mistake, but for a long time I refused to acknowledge it.

If Desmond noticed I was upset, he didn't mention it. Instead, he told me that he had to go out for a while that evening.

'I have some goods I need to take to a safe place. I'd take you with me, but I've a colleague coming too and the car will be full. I expect you will enjoy watching television anyway.'

Somehow, I managed to put on a smile and tell him I would. I was used to various explanations about his work but eventually I was to find out that it was all a bundle of lies. As with many liars, part of what he told me did have some truth in it. When the evening came I saw him changing into black trousers and the same colour shirt before he gave me a kiss and left, saying he would see me later. Over the next hour or so I found myself missing my family home so much that, when I climbed into bed, I cried myself to sleep.

Desmond woke me up when I felt him crawling into bed. His arm went round me as he held me against his body. I went stiff for a few moments but, much to my relief, he didn't try to have sex with me that night. That made me relax and I fell asleep in his arms.

When I woke in the morning, I was on my own in the

bed. Desmond saw my eyes opening and brought me over a cup of tea.

'Thought you needed to rest a little,' he said as he placed it by my side of the bed before leaning over and giving me a kiss.

'Here's a dressing gown for you,' he said.

It was a really pretty pink-and-white one.

'You'll need it when you want to go to the loo,' he told me. 'Oh, and here's a little present for you as well …'

A bottle of expensive perfume appeared next to my tea.

That was enough for me to feel that the love I had for him was returned and my whole body tingled with pleasure.

41

My grandmother phoned me the next day: 'Where are you, Georgia?'

I didn't exactly tell her, I just said that I was at a friend's place.

'Don't be silly,' she told me. 'I read your note and, of course, you must come back home. You have college to get ready for, don't you?'

With all the drama, I had almost forgotten about the course I was due to start. I told her that I would get ready and go straight there. She asked me again if I wouldn't prefer being at home but, being a stubborn and somewhat emotional teenager, I told her that I was all right where I was. I could hear the annoyance in her voice when she insisted that she believed I would be better at home. I can't blame her for feeling pretty angry and now I know that she was worried about me.

So, I started college and I was really getting excited about the course I had chosen, but just a few weeks later, my period didn't come. By that time, I was convinced that Desmond and

I were very close. My nervousness about sleeping with him disappeared after our first night of making love. He was a gentle lover then, one who knew how to make me want to be with him every hour of the day. I suspect he was ensuring that I became hooked on him.

I didn't tell Desmond about my period, just that I needed to get a few things from the chemist. I managed to go in on my own and get a pregnancy kit. Once back, I dashed to the toilet and just about forced myself to pee. I sat on the toilet anxiously waiting for the result. Two coloured lines appeared within ten minutes, which according to the instructions – which I read over and over again – told me I was pregnant.

My morning sickness began soon after that, which stopped me going to college. First, I told them it was flu and then I made up another excuse. Of course, they then wanted a doctor's note, which stopped me making any more excuses. Was I pleased I was pregnant? Not really, it would put a stop to my education and we were not living in a place suitable for a baby.

I kept telling myself everything would be all right. After all, ever since I was about ten or even younger, I had dreamt of having my own family. Seems that's a dream that many little girls have. They certainly don't picture having their husband and a baby living in one room in a dingy hostel, though.

When I knew there was a baby growing inside my body, I felt both depressed and confused. It seemed only yesterday that I was starting my periods and, still a virgin when I left home, now I was going to be a mother. I kept telling myself that everything would be all right – Desmond would find us somewhere comfortable to live and then we would be a family. Would Nan be all right about my pregnancy? I missed her terribly. She might be out of touch with my generation but her love for me was without question.

While I was thinking of her, my phone rang and I recognised the number: it was Nan. I fervently hoped it was a friendly call, but it wasn't. She had been informed by the college that I appeared to have left the course. I took a deep breath and spluttered out the reason I couldn't study any more. There was silence and I held my breath, waiting for her to say something.

She did, but it was not what I had wished to hear.

42

Nan got off the phone so fast that I could tell she was really angry. Now I think she was more dismayed by what she had heard. It was a good thing that Desmond was out that morning as I would hardly have wanted him hearing what she had to say on the phone.

With hindsight, I should have waited for her to take in the news and then rung her back, but back then I believed there would be no point in doing that or trying to see her. I was so miserable – she was the person I missed the most every single day.

I still hadn't told Desmond that I was pregnant, which worried me. The question that I was struggling with was, how would he would accept becoming a father? Would he be as annoyed as my nan was? Or might he accuse me of already being pregnant by another man before I left home? As I ran how the scenario might play out, I imagined him throwing all my belongings into my suitcase and telling me to go back home.

When he arrived back from work, I knew I had to tell him. I clenched my fists so tightly that my nails went into my skin as I blurted out, 'I'm pregnant, Desmond.'

'Wow, Georgia! I can't believe it,' he said and a huge grin came onto his face. He put his arms around me and gave me such a huge hug that I nearly cried with joy and relief.

'I hope it's a boy, although I'd love a little girl as well,' he told me.

That made me so relieved and I was glowing with happiness. I waited for him to tell me that we would get somewhere with a second bedroom, but he never said a word about it. Instead, he told me that we couldn't stay in the hostel any longer as our room had been booked by someone else, who was due to move in soon.

'Sorry, Georgia, I forgot the date, so we have to leave tomorrow. Still, I've already found a place for us to go to. It's near my mother and sister. Mum left my dad years ago, in case you were wondering. My mum and sister will be so pleased when they meet you. I'll go and see them first and let Mum know she's going to be a grandmother – that will make her happy.'

Of course, I still hoped that he was going to tell me that he would be looking for a flat, one with a small second bedroom with a cot in it. That was my dream, a new life with the three of us in it. That picture shattered as I heard him say it was another bedsit with a shared kitchen, toilet and bathroom. 'Just temporary, until we can get a better place,' he told me.

'You mean we'll have a larger place to live in before our baby is born?' I wanted to know.

'We will, so don't fret. We have a few months to go, haven't we?'

'Yes, I suppose we have,' I agreed, though that didn't stop me from feeling disappointed.

The following morning, we packed up our things and were ready to leave an hour or so later. Desmond didn't let me pick up my case. 'Just bring those carrier bags of yours, you can't go carrying anything heavy,' he said, which made me feel rather proud as we walked out together.

There were a few people at the front of the building, but Desmond certainly didn't want to stop and talk to anyone, so I followed him as briskly as I could. He piled everything quickly into the car and opened the door for me once I had put my carrier bags in the boot.

'Come on, get straight in,' he told me.

As he drove off, I was just hoping the place would be better than the one we had been staying in. I rested my head on the back of the seat and watched the roads that we passed on our way to North Finchley. I was quite sleepy when he pulled up in front of a large block. 'We're here,' he said. Opening my eyes, I saw another building which hardly appeared to be clean or bright. The moment I entered, I could see it was even worse inside. Everywhere I looked, it seemed grimy. I couldn't understand why Desmond had not tried to rent something a lot better. He had always given me the impression that not only did his father give him an allowance, but he also earned good money. The sight of his flashy car had confirmed my opinion but for some reason it had now disappeared and he was driving a bit of an old banger.

'Borrowed my sister's car,' had been his explanation when he saw me looking a bit surprised. 'I'll be getting another one soon. That will be much better than this old thing.'

Personally, I would rather have travelled on buses or tubes and have him use the money for us to live in a decent place. After all, he had wanted me to live with him, but had avoided telling me what it would be like.

'We'll get something better soon,' he told me as we walked into the bedsit.

I certainly hoped so. It took us a whole day to get it looking vaguely clean. We had the window open wide to let in some fresh air. Luckily, Desmond had brought his own bedding and towels.

It didn't take long for me to find out that most of the people there were on benefits and no one appeared interested in getting work. Still, that was none of my business, except with my early life experiences, I recognised a lot of the signs indicating our neighbours were drug addicts. No wonder I hated it there. I can remember how I felt when I realised that the woman next door to us was definitely a crack head. She kept hanging around our room, waiting for one of us to come out. I only had to open the door and there she was. It was drugs she wanted and, for some reason, she thought I would have some.

'I don't take anything like that,' I told her.

She cackled with laughter at that.

'You don't?'

She smiled knowingly and wandered away.

I can still picture what living there was like and how

much I disliked it. My memory recoils as I think about that woman, with her greasy hair, black rotting teeth and scabby skin. She freaked me out every time I saw her – I suppose it brought back so many memories of my experiences with my mother's 'friends'.

Desmond knew that I hated it and kept telling me that we wouldn't be staying there for long – 'Just a short while and then we'll move again.'

He didn't explain what he meant.

A few days later, he went to visit his mum and sister. He had gone without me as no doubt he wanted to talk to them about me, although I had no idea about what he was saying.

'I don't have to work till a bit late,' he told me. 'How about we all meet at a cafe for coffee afterwards?'

With her long dark hair and deep-brown eyes, Chanel seemed really friendly to me. She must have been a few years younger than her brother and I took to her straight away, but I couldn't say the same for Desmond's mother. There was something about the way she scrutinised me that made me feel uncomfortable.

We all had coffee and then Desmond said he and his mother had some shopping to do in the supermarket just up the road, so Chanel and I could carry on chatting.

'Order yourselves some food, I'll pay when I come back.'

Of course, I had no idea then that leaving me with his sister was the first part of his planned strategy. Once they had left, Chanel said, 'Desmond told me that neither of you want to stay in the place you've moved into. I'll try and help you find somewhere else. How does that sound?'

'A lot better,' I said.

'The best thing is for us to go to the council. I know you're pregnant, Desmond told us, and Mum and I are thrilled. I'll be an aunt, and Mum a grandmother. She's excited about that. The council will want to help when we tell them that. I can go to the phone box over the road and make an appointment, what do you think?'

I couldn't stop myself from blurting out, 'Anything to get us out of that place!'

If Chanel was taken aback at this remark, she didn't show it.

'Good! The best thing is for me to take you to the council without Desmond: two girls would work better than a good-looking man with his girlfriend. Being pregnant will also help. Let them think it's only you, otherwise they might say that a man with a job can afford to rent in the private sector. This might well be a chance of getting a flat.'

'Sounds a great idea, thank you so much,' I told her.

I watched as she left the cafe and walked over to the phone box. I could see the phone in her hand and her lips moving. A few minutes after she had talked and listened, she hung up and came and sat with me, a big smile on her face.

'We've got an appointment!'

What I didn't know was that the phone call was only a pretend one and that the appointment had already been made. I never found out if Chanel knew the man we were about to see – I suspect she did as I soon discovered that she had a knack for making friends who might be useful to her. The pair of us ordered some food and more coffee while we waited for

Desmond and his mother to return. Once they did, Chanel told him about the appointment. He played his part well and appeared a little resentful: 'Surely it's up to me and not Georgia to see them?'

'Oh, come on, Desmond! She looks so young and pretty, they're more likely to want to help her get some safe accommodation and that will be good for both of you,' his sister said.

He put an arm around my shoulder and looked into my face: 'Are you all right about going there with Chanel and not me? You've never had to do anything like that before, have you?'

'I'm fine,' I told him. 'I'll tell them I'm pregnant – Chanel says that will help. Don't want pregnant girls sleeping on the streets, do they?'

He laughed out loud at this: 'Don't think that would happen to you.'

Even though he seemed affectionate towards me, I still thought he would rather have gone himself. That, I realised a few weeks later, was what he wanted me to believe.

What I had no idea of then was that Desmond couldn't risk having anything in his name. He and his family all knew that there was a warrant for his arrest, so he had to lie low. In fact, I later found out that was the real reason we had to leave the previous place: Desmond had lied to me about someone having it booked. He had actually found out that the police were looking for him in all the residential places like that.

Shrewdly, he never gave anyone his address. He had also been careful not to tell anyone at the first hostel where we were going, but there weren't that many similar places. For me to get a place in my name might just save him being arrested. What he didn't remember was that there were people in the first place who knew my name as well as his. Somebody there had asked me my name and, not knowing it could cause a problem, I had naively given it.

Even before we moved again, I was beginning to see the other side of Desmond. The side I was innocent enough to accept his and Chanel's excuses for. That evening, he made a bit of fuss about a place being put in my name, though as I've said, I would soon realise that this was only a pretence. He needed somewhere to stay where no one, especially the landlord, knew his name.

Both his mother and sister had already denied that they had seen him and knew where he was; not that the police believed them. Neither of them had a good reputation and his mother was a known shoplifter. Although her daughter had been with her on a number of occasions, nothing could be proven against her. His mother was lucky as, so far, she had just got a ticking-off.

I was not to find any of this out for some time.

When Chanel came round in the morning, I was up and waited for her. She had the key to the car and drove us to the council offices. When we went in, we were met by a young man who told us that our appointment was with him. He took us to a spot where there were some chairs and a small table. He had a file in his hand with my name on the cover.

To begin with, Chanel did all the talking and she told him a little about my childhood and how terrible it had been.

'Now she's pregnant and her boyfriend has disappeared, but she couldn't stay with her mother, could she? Not with all the druggies about.'

'I suppose not, after what you have just told me,' he said.

Talk about being a good liar! Chanel was certainly accomplished and left out the fact that I had lived with my grandparents for seven years and had two aunts who would have helped if I went to them. There was no doubt that my grandparents would have taken me back if they had been asked. But, of course, Desmond would not be welcome.

The man, whose name I have not put in my story, looked as though he felt very sorry for me.

'The baby will arrive soon,' Chanel said, 'and she's not got anywhere to go to. I could put her up on our two-seater sofa for a while but that wouldn't be good for her or the baby, would it?'

He looked as though he appreciated the severity of every word she said.

At the end of our interview, I was offered a bedsitter in Edmonton, north London, and I could move in the next day – 'It's in a small block so it will be quiet.' That sounded a little better. To my delight, the man said that I would also go on the list for a small flat and he was fairly certain that I would be able to move in before the baby came.

After our interview finished, we went to a coffee shop to relax a little. I could hardly stop thanking Chanel, but she just smiled and said she was pleased for us.

Once we arrived back home, both of us noticed that Desmond had packed nearly all our belongings up and left the room looking clean and tidy. I thought he must have done this to please me as he had seemed rather bad-tempered when I left with Chanel that morning.

'I wonder where he is?'

We couldn't find Desmond anywhere in the block and so we knocked on the doors of most of the people he had made friends with. I decided to knock on the druggie woman's door just in case she knew. She opened the door and replied, 'Who's Desmond?' then slammed it shut.

Chanel told me something wasn't right and started banging on her door. With that, the woman shouted, 'I gave him a blowjob, all right?'

I was so shocked that I couldn't even speak.

'She's just trying to upset you, Georgia,' Chanel said. 'He wouldn't touch a dirty bitch like that, would he?'

Finally, we caught up with Desmond in one of the corridors. He must have been coming back to the room but he was white as a ghost. Straight away, I noticed that his pupils were enlarged. My heart sank. I had seen enough of those signs when I was seven years younger. Up until then, I had never realised he took drugs. On top of what the woman had said and seeing the state he was in, I felt my temper rise and just about spat out that enough was enough, I was going straight back to Nan's. Without saying anything, his leg went up and he kicked me straight in the stomach. I doubled up, choking, and Chanel caught hold of me before I collapsed.

'I'm going to take you back to the room so you can just sit there for a few minutes. I want to talk to my brother and then I'll come and get you,' she told me, before adding,

'You stay there, Desmond.' She put her arm around my waist and walked me to the room.

'He's on drugs, isn't he?' I said. 'I can't stand them – I've watched them wreck people's lives, including mine.'

'Oh, it's not like him, Georgia,' she told me. 'I think someone gave him something – he's worried about his work.'

Well, that part was true as Desmond's work had caused at least one warrant for his arrest to be out. Chanel carried on saying that maybe he foolishly took it because of his work worries: 'That's what made him act so differently.'

Didn't she notice that I was in a complete mess? Had that dreadful woman told the truth? And then, when I confronted Desmond about taking drugs, he kicked at our baby – the one he said he wanted so much. After all, I had given up everything to be with him. Was my life with him going to be a repeat of my yearly years?

'I want to go now, Chanel,' I said.

'Let me talk to him, just wait a little and do some deep breathing,' she told me.

I know I should have gone, but I agreed to this. I don't know what she said to him, but he apologised as soon as Chanel came to get me.

'I shouldn't have taken it,' he told me, meaning the drugs. 'I was just so uptight and one of the guys here gave me a tablet. I won't ever do it again, Georgia.'

Although I had been wary of addicts from when I was much younger, I hadn't yet learnt that serious drugs were not in tablet form, so that was another lie. Like the young foolish girl I was, I forgave him. He gave me a hug and later on the next day, we moved into the bedsit, where I was met by the man from the council. When he gave me the keys and left, I went to the car to fetch Desmond – he had parked around the corner so he wouldn't be spotted.

The place was nice and clean, and it had a small kitchen and a tiny bathroom. Staying there was both calm and friendly but, sadly, short-lived. We had only been there for a couple of weeks when there was a hammering on the door in the middle of the night.

'I'm going to hide in the bathroom,' he whispered. 'You tell those people you're here on your own.'

I called out that I would open the door when I put my dressing gown on – I could tell they had no intention of leaving. When I opened up, two policemen were standing outside.

'Good thing you opened the door or we would have kicked it down,' the taller of the two said as they pushed me aside and entered.

'So, where is he?'

'Who?'

'Stop playing games, girlie – you know who.'

The police officer walked straight over to the bathroom and, with one solid kick, the door flew open. He pulled Desmond out, stated his name and told him he was being arrested for theft. It all took less than a minute and I stood there, watching him being cuffed and marched out the door.

43

I was about four months pregnant when I heard that Desmond was being released from prison. Chanel suggested that I stay the night with her as his mother wanted to see him first and it would be good if I was also there waiting for him. I agreed to this and went over to them the night before so that I would be there when he arrived.

'I wanted to pick him up,' Chanel told me, 'but he said he had a few things to do before he came here.'

It was just after midday when he finally arrived and I was shocked at his appearance. I could tell by his eyes that it was drugs he had wanted to collect before he went home and that he had already taken some. I shuddered a little as I had perhaps naively thought that, after being in prison, he would be clean. Since I was a young child, I had seen how drugs can change a nice person into someone I didn't like.

I forced myself to smile at him as I said, 'I'm so happy you're here now,' and moved towards him, expecting a hug.

But I didn't get one; he had no intention of wrapping his arms around me. Instead, he glared in my direction and accused me of being with other men while he was away.

'You have, haven't you?'

'What?! When I have your baby inside me?'

'So, why are you all done up? Makes you look as though you're nothing but a slut.'

'Who on earth put those ideas into your head?' his sister exclaimed. 'Been listening to men in your unit who have never even met her, have you?'

But that didn't stop him slapping my face hard in front of Chanel, which almost made me fall over. Then more insults came my way about what he thought I'd been up to.

His sister caught hold of his arm and ticked him off. I could tell by the way he appeared dazed that the drugs were working in his head. Should I have left then? I should have told myself I would be stupid if I didn't. My one excuse for staying was that I was only 17. It was as if there was an invisible rope tied between us that he could pull on at will and stop me walking away.

I suppose deep down I still wanted to be part of a happy family. That was the dream I had nurtured for so long. I remembered how I told my sister that I had a picture in my head of Desmond and I walking hand in hand across a beach or a meadow as we discussed names for our baby.

'I know you love him, but think why he kept moving from hostel to hostel. It was because there was a warrant out for him and he lied to you. Don't let that man ruin your life, Georgia,' Lucy told me firmly. 'Think how our mother married a good-looking man who was unfaithful, stole money from her and her father, and ended up beating her up.'

That advice that was now pushed to the back of my young mind, where it stayed far too long.

As I stood there shaking, he put his arm round me and, before I could shrug him off, he apologised. Told me he had worried all the time that I might have started seeing someone else while he was away: 'My sister's right, the men in there were teasing me about you. Said I couldn't count on you being faithful to me. I'm so sorry I lost my temper like that.'

Chanel gave a sigh of relief. His mother, who no doubt had been listening, came out then and told us to come and sit down as she was bringing out some tea. She didn't ask any questions about what he was going to do next, just kept smiling and saying she was so pleased to see him back.

After about an hour or so Desmond and I left and went back to the bedsit. I thought that he would be pleased that I had managed to buy his favourite foods as well as a couple of beers. He certainly thanked me enough. The rest of that day was a lot better than when he had arrived. By the time we snuggled up together in bed, I was really happy to have him back – he seemed to be the same person that I had first shared a bed with.

The following day was not one that kept me feeling safe and loved, however, and by the end of it, I was very uneasy. The day started well – we had gone out together in the afternoon to do some grocery shopping and, when we got back, he told me he needed a rest and went to lie down on the bed. A little later I heard his phone ring and saw him putting it up to his ear. All I heard him say was 'all right' and then he threw it down in a temper. I could tell straight away that whatever the person on the phone had said had put Desmond in a black mood, one that would inevitably make him turn on me.

'I can't stand the way you were walking when we were out,' was his opening remark.

'I can hardly help that, Desmond, I'm nearly five months pregnant,' I told him.

'Oh, so that's your excuse, is it?' he said before firing off other small insults at me – that I spoke too much one moment and not enough the next, and I wore too much make-up, which made me look common.

Actually, I never wore that much, but I decided not to provoke him and kept quiet, though he was now shouting out his insults. I did my best not to let him make me cry.

'I've got to go out now,' he said as he jumped off the bed. He pulled on a jacket, went through the door and slammed it behind him. Him leaving for a while was quite a relief to me – I just hoped he would be in a better mood when he came back, but I doubted it.

I was still awake when he came back in the early hours of the morning, but I pretended to be asleep and, as soon as I heard his heavy breathing, I knew he was sound asleep. I couldn't stand the smell of alcohol on his breath and, as soon as he started to snore, I got out of bed. I had heard him drop something on the bedside table when he came in and so I went to have a look.

I saw a whole collection of things he must have stolen from somewhere. There were mobile phones, a digital camera as well as a wad of money, all of which he had tossed down carelessly, making no attempt to conceal them from me. I found myself looking through the photos on the camera. It was then that I recognised a girl who had been in the same school as me. It wasn't just what was going through my mind, but my gut also told me straight away that something was very wrong.

It must have been me getting out of bed that woke him and, as I looked up, I realised he was sitting up in bed and watching me.

'Did you steal these things?'

'Oh, stop being so paranoid, Georgia,' he shouted and then lay back down and, thankfully, fell back to sleep.

Just as I finished looking through the photos on the camera, my phone rang. It was four in the morning so I couldn't understand who would ring me at that early hour. But I picked it up and heard Desmond's mother's voice screaming down the phone that her son was wanted by the police for rape.

'I don't believe it,' she kept saying. 'Some stupid girl has told them that and the police are looking for him now. He must have turned his phone off, so wake him up and let me speak to him. I have to let him know that he needs to disappear for a while.'

Desmond must have heard the phone and woken up.

'It's your mother,' I said as I passed it to him.

I heard him saying that it was a lie and that she had offered him sex, but then I heard him agree that he would do as she suggested. I managed to be calm and, thankfully, so did he. He told to me he had gone to a house party after an argument with his friend. Yes, he had sex with the girl in the photo, that I already knew.

'And no, there was no rape – it was her who clung to me and dragged me into a bedroom. We were both pretty drunk, but she made it clear from the start that she fancied me.'

He told me all this as though none of it mattered or might upset me.

'So, what did you do that annoyed her so much?'

'OK, I admit I did help myself to a few things in the house. To get her own back, she probably thought that accusing me of rape would be of more interest to the police than my pinching a couple of phones. Anyhow, all the stuff's insured.'

I believed him – I couldn't see him as a rapist.

'She might not go ahead with the charges against me. I don't think she'll want to be examined by a doctor. If she was, there wouldn't be any proof on her body showing she was forced, no bruises or marks. As it happened at a party, how come no one heard her shrieking for help? She loved it! But I'll go to a mate's house now until I find out what's happening. I sure don't want to be thrown in a cell again,' he told me as he began pulling on his clothes. He picked the money up, then threw down a couple of ten-pound notes.

'You can put them in your purse, should help you a bit.'

I just looked at them blankly and felt like saying that I didn't want stolen money. But by then I felt as if I was going mad. How could he come back from prison, leave me, go to a party, steal stuff and then have sex with a girl about my age? Was it the shape caused by my pregnancy that made him turn his back on me? I felt so messed up emotionally and a depression descended on me as soon as he walked out; I could hardly believe that, yet again, he was on the run from the police.

After a few weeks, the police did arrest him. He was taken to the station but was told no further action was being taken, which meant they had dismissed the charge of rape. Of course, as you will probably guess, I was foolish enough to forgive him and take him back again.

44

One thing that pleased me was that the council had stuck to their word and given me a one-bedroom flat on a reasonable estate. The rooms were small, but it was a lot better for us and my unborn baby than the bedsit. I really thought that this was our chance to settle down and that Desmond would begin to behave as he had at the beginning of our relationship. I still longed to have the family of my own that I had dreamt of and I so desperately didn't want to be a teenage single mum.

After a while I got in contact with my nan again, as well as my dad. He came over to see me, took one look at the flat and told me he would get some paint and make it look much better.

'You could give me a hand,' he told Desmond and received a friendly smile in response. They had met a few times and seemed to get on.

Dad turned up the next day with cans of white and pale-pink paint. After making them some coffee and the three of us chatting a bit, they began to paint the flat. Once most of the work was done and the place was looking pretty smart, Desmond made excuses to go out. I just knew that he was cheating on me again – it was the smell of aftershave that told me that it was not work he was up to. But I said nothing. It was when he had left our flat a few more times that I told him I knew about his cheating. That was enough for him to tell me again that I was paranoid. His persistent use of the word was starting to make me doubt myself.

But it was the drug-taking that really frightened me. They changed him into a different person, one that I was scared of. There was another night when he told me he was going out and I invited my friend Kirsty over. I mentioned it to him, but I don't think it sank in.

Just before he left the flat, he began rowing with me. The scorn in his voice when he shouted at me meant that it was the worst argument since we had moved in. His temper fired up and, snarling with rage, he kicked me so hard, I fell against the door. It hadn't been closed properly and I flew out of it backwards. That happened just as my friend was coming up the stairs to meet me. She helped me up and took me into our living room.

Desmond gave her a dirty look and then stormed out of the flat.

Kirsty got me to lie down on the small sofa and made me some sweet tea as I was very shaky.

'Look, Georgia, you have to leave that man. Or, as it's your flat, get the police to get him out. It's your name on the lease, not his. Think of your baby, he's due in just a few weeks. I can honestly tell you that I have never seen a temper like that.

You must know he's dangerous. If you had fallen down those stairs, I doubt if you would still be pregnant. Now what are you going to do?' she said.

'I'll go to Nan's,' I told her.

'Good for you! You should stay there for a while. I'll pack some of your clothes up for you while you ring your grandmother, then I'll get us a cab and take you there.'

*   *   *

Nan had always told me that I was welcome to come back any time. She knew I was pregnant, which I doubt pleased her, but she never said so. I phoned her and, without telling her why, I asked if I could stay with them for a while.

Heavily pregnant, and completely drained, I really needed to be in the house that had been my home for so long. Kirsty did as she promised and a small suitcase appeared by my side as she called for a taxi. She came in with me for a short while, had some tea with Nan and then left.

Over the time I spent there, Nan went out of her way to make me feel relaxed and welcome. During the first few days, I was able to rest as it was so peaceful there. My brother Sid chatted to me, and if he knew the details about Desmond, he didn't say. I guess, as he had been in the police force for some time, he must have been aware of the sort of man I was involved with.

It was on the about the fifth evening that Desmond turned up at the house, screaming my name and throwing things at the windows. Luckily, Sid was in at the time. He marched out of the front door and, after taking one look at his muscular frame, Desmond turned and ran.

After that had happened several times, I told Nan that I had a friend I could stay with. I had learnt about Grandad's dementia by then and all the commotion was upsetting him; he became very agitated each time it occurred. It was so sad to see that he was no longer the man he had been. A few years earlier he would have stormed out himself and made Desmond fear for his life.

I made a call to another old school friend, Niki, and asked if I could stay there as she had often invited me over. She said, 'Hang on a second,' and I heard her ask her mum, Carol, if that was all right. In the background I heard Carol saying, 'Yes, of course, tell her to come straight away.'

After I had finished that call, I received another one from Kirsty, who had gone to pick up a few more things for me at the flat. She wanted to let me know she had managed to get what I wanted but it hadn't been easy: when she went in, there were Desmond and Chanel, busy smashing everything to pieces. They had also written in huge letters on one of the recently painted walls, 'Why did you leave me?'

As I had believed that Chanel was a friend, I felt sickened by her actions.

'I thought she was your friend too,' Kirsty said, 'but she clearly adores her brother and I know a bit about her – she also has a crooked streak and only helped you to please him. I've always told you Desmond's dangerous and I'm right. When you go back, get some very strong locks on that door – I'm sure I could help you sort it out.'

'I don't know if I could stay there now,' I told her miserably.

I then told her that I couldn't stay at Nan's any longer because of Desmond upsetting my grandfather – 'Niki says I can stay with her and her mum while I sort my head out.'

'Keep in touch and let me know how you're getting on,' she told me.

45

That night, I went over to Niki's and was made so welcome. I rang my sister from there to explain what had happened. She, in turn, got hold of Dad the next day and told him all about it. He agreed that he would fix everything up and change the locks to the flat while I stayed with Niki and her Mum Carol.

I will never forget the terrible day when, having reached my nine months of pregnancy, I wet myself. It was Desmond who caused it. I can remember hearing a knock on the door and Carol went to open it. She must have been shocked when she saw who it was standing outside. As she tried to slam it shut, Desmond jammed his boot in the gap; his fist flew towards her face and sent her flying. Niki tried to stop him coming near me, which made him thump her hard in the ribs. I ran into another room and tried to lock the door, but he kicked it open and got in. I could barely recognise his face – it had the most vicious expression on it that I had ever seen. That was when I wet myself in fear.

'You shouldn't have left me,' I heard him say before his

fist flew into my body again and again. I started screaming as it was the worst beating he had ever given me. There was blood pouring from my nose, my mouth was also full of blood and, to my horror, there was blood trickling between my legs. I thought he was trying to kill me and our baby as well.

Carol shouted out that she had called the police, telling them there was an attempted murder of a pregnant woman taking place in her house.

'They're sending an armed response unit, they'll be here in a minute and they'll have guns!'

Hearing that was enough for Desmond to land one more punch on me before he ran to the door and left.

I was almost unconscious but, in the distance, I could hear Carol saying that there was an ambulance on the way. The medics arrived very quickly and I was put on a stretcher and rushed to hospital, where I was given painkillers and a scan. It was the nurse holding my hand who reassured me that my baby was all right, which made me feel so relieved.

'Your baby's going to come very soon, so we're taking you to the maternity unit,' she told me as she and a male nurse wheeled me to a single room in a wheelchair.

I did wonder how Desmond had found out where I was. It might have been through my dad, who having had a few drinks after he had fixed everything, had told Desmond about Niki. Dad never came to visit me while I was in hospital, nor did I ever see him again, for he simply disappeared. All I know is that he was mixing with some pretty dodgy people at the time.

46

It was Nan who rushed to the hospital after she had been told the baby would be born later that day. I had been asked about my next-of-kin and had given them Nan's name and phone number. She was determined to sit beside me and encourage me during the birth. Like many other mothers, I really don't remember the pain of giving birth.

My beautiful son arrived in the world at 4.15 p.m. on 26 September 2006.

'It's a boy!' I heard the midwife say as I was helped up a little. After he was cleaned and weighed, he was placed in my arms. I could hardly believe he was here at last; I was so completely fascinated as to how I had created such an amazing and beautiful child. Finally, I had someone I could love unconditionally, and I felt that he would love me back.

Nan also thought he was beautiful, but she gave nothing away about her thoughts on his father. I made sure that she didn't hear about the beating he had given me; I had asked Carol not to tell her, saying Nan had enough anxiety already about Grandad's dementia and I didn't want her to have any more worries.

'I didn't give the police his name,' Carol told me. 'Though if he appears anywhere near you again, you should open a case of assault against him.'

I was on a ward proudly holding my newborn child and thinking everything had just become perfect but then the doctor told me there was a problem with my son that managed to dampen my happiness: he had to be put on a special unit as he needed antibiotics for a blood problem. As the doctors were aware of what had happened to me before I came into hospital, I was allowed to stay in a little longer.

I was able to sit in the unit most of the time he was there. It must have been three days after he was born when a nurse approached me. 'I think you should take a nap,' she said. 'You're looking very tired.'

I insisted that I was all right, but to be truthful, I was exhausted so I gave in to her and went back to my room. I must have slept for at least 30 minutes and then, not wanting to rest any more, I decided to go back to my baby. It was then that I saw an armed policeman outside my door. That made me get up immediately and ask, 'What are you doing here?' I was thinking something awful must be happening in the hospital. 'My baby's still in the unit, isn't he?'

Naturally, that was my first reaction.

'No, Miss, not now,' he replied bluntly, 'he's been taken to an emergency foster home. Your partner threatened to kidnap both you and your son by coming in here with a shotgun. By the way, he wanted you to know he would get you.

This will add to his jail sentence, seeing as there's another warrant out for him.'

I tried to say that, as bad as Desmond could be, he would never have meant that. He was only sending a nasty message for me.

'Maybe, but he still made that threat,' the police officer said.

He then told me that they also had to remove me from the hospital as a matter of urgency. The policeman didn't say that I would be taken to a women's refuge, instead I was to be taken to one of my Dad's sisters, Aunt Ellen, who had agreed for me to stay with her. It didn't take long for me to find myself being bundled out of the hospital, armed with medication to stop me lactating, put in a police car and then, childless and confused, I was driven to my aunt's house.

Goodness knows how Desmond found out where I was again. He must have guessed which aunt I would be staying with. As she was Dad's sister, it could be that my father had talked about her and mentioned where she lived. Or was it someone else who had told him where I was? I never did find out. But then there are still quite a few things in my life that I haven't discovered the answers to. Especially the mystery surrounding Dad, who as I said, just disappeared from our lives. No one knew where he had gone or why he never told us where he was going.

* * *

All I can remember is that, after my aunt had gone out, it only took a few minutes before I heard Desmond knocking on the door. No doubt he had been hiding near the house and had waited to see when she was going out. He was calling out my name and pleading for me to please listen to him.

I was frozen in fear. What I should have done was to pick up the phone and call the police. But no, I didn't. When I didn't answer him, he phoned me on my mobile, which I foolishly answered. Of course, he was too cunning to sound angry – I think he must have learnt some acting from his famous father, for he managed to sound so concerned about his son and me. He asked if Matthew was with me and said he couldn't wait to see him.

I should have told him that his threat had caused all the problems and that was why Matthew was not with me. As soon as I got off the call, I should have switched off my phone. Instead, I went to the door and opened it. I can hardly believe that my younger self was so naive to do that. Or should I say stupid.

One look at his face told me I had made a huge mistake: there was a mixture of triumph and anger all over it. Wanting to get away from him, I tried to step back into the house, but his plan must have been to make me feel sorry enough for him to open the door. Before I could even step back in, his hand shot out, grabbed the neck of my jumper and pulled me outside.

'Help, help!' I yelled, hoping one of the neighbours would hear me, but it seemed that no one did.

He dragged me to his car, which I could tell was a stolen one, and threw me in. The door was slammed shut and locked. I felt so frightened when he got in beside me and started the engine, determined not to let me go. I told him that my aunt would be very worried when she came back to the house and saw I wasn't there.

No comment.

I then asked where he was taking me to, which made him punch me hard – 'Don't keep asking questions, you'll find out when we get there.' Even when he was driving quite fast, he still managed to punch me hard a couple more times; he kept telling me it was my fault *his* son, not ours, had been taken into foster care.

'I know why they took him away – it's because they could tell you would be a useless mother. That's the reason they took him off you.'

There was no point in arguing – I knew if I did, his fist would land hard on my body again. Besides, his cruel words were just as painful.

It must have been well over an hour before Desmond turned the car into a lane in a bleak part of the countryside. He pulled up in a small, deserted woodland area where we wouldn't be seen by anyone on the road. My heart sank. My phone was still in my hand and I was trying to hide it under my clothing, but he must have noticed it when he threw me in the car. A bullying smirk appeared on his face when he managed to prise it from my hands and then smashed it as hard as he could against the car door.

'Now, you can forget about trying to make calls,' he told me.

I shivered with fright: what was he going to do to me?

'I'm going to get us some food,' he told me, 'and you'd better behave when I leave you in the car.'

I said nothing as he drove to a shop, which was next to a small chemist. All the time I prayed silently that there would be people about who could help me. I might have known that he was pretty sure there would not be cars at the back of the shops because that's where he parked. There was not one in sight, which told me there was little hope of being rescued.

Don't cry, I told myself, *that will only please him.*

Milk was still coming from my breasts, which told me I needed some breast pads pretty soon. The hospital had given me loads but, of course, they had been left behind. But he just laughed at me when I asked if he would get some from the chemist.

'You shouldn't have lost my son,' he said as he got out of the car and locked me in again.

He came out of the shop fairly quickly and threw a large plastic bag containing bread, cheese and bottled water onto the back seat before driving back to the wooded area. At least he let me eat and drink water from the bottles he had bought.

When I asked, he walked me into the woods and let me pee behind a bush – he knew there was no chance of me running off in my condition. That first night, we stayed in the car, though I hardly slept. The next morning, he told me we would stay in a B&B and that, if I tried to say anything to the owner, I would regret it.

So I didn't.

The time with him was truly devastating. When there was no one about, his fists rained down on me several times. It was all about 'my son' and the anger that I had left him that kept making him want to hurt me. After that second night, to my relief, he told me we were going back to London.

Just after he stopped the car on one of the main roads, he turned to me and asked, 'Are your boobs still sore after having the baby?' Before I could answer, he punched me straight in my breast. It was so painful, I nearly passed out. He then opened the car door and pushed me out. Although my body felt sore and my legs were shaky, all I could think was that I was finally free.

It was about three in the morning and pouring with rain but still I could hear him shouting, 'Fuck you! Go and get my kid back!' Sore as I was, I began running with tears streaming down my face. I had hardly got far when I heard the sound of his feet behind me. Although I tried to outrun him, Desmond had longer legs than mine and once again I felt his hands clutching hold of my shoulders.

'You really think I would let you go, you crazy bitch? I own you!' he shrieked before hitting me again.

'That hurts, doesn't it, Georgia? Well, you hurt me when you tried to leave me. My sister and my mum think you're such an unfaithful person.'

A little piece of luck came my way then: it was the sight of a police car coming in our direction. Desmond must have known there was another warrant out for him and his dread of police cells made him run off. As the police car didn't even slow down, I didn't think it was out looking for him at all. Which made me scared. I thought that, once he saw the police car had gone, he might begin looking for me again.

Now I dived into a side street as fast as I could. I was

looking for a telephone box so that I could make a call but they were few and far between. Once I had managed to do that, I would begin to feel safer. I had a few coins in my pocket. Desmond hadn't noticed that I had taken some of the ones he had left on the dressing table in the B&B – good thing he was always so careless with coins.

Finally, I found a telephone box and managed to phone Carol. Although I must have woken her up, she sounded so pleased to hear from me. Nan had told her that she believed I had been kidnapped by Desmond – she knew I wouldn't have gone missing from my aunt's house unless I had been forced to.

Carol told me to stay where I was and she would drive over and pick me up. 'Your nan's so worried about you,' she told me. 'She believes that crazy Desmond managed to get you out of the house.'

'He did,' I told her.

It seemed like an age before she arrived. Just in case Desmond drove down that street, I hid behind a hedge in someone's garden, shaking. I was so relieved when I saw Carol's car pulling up. As I came out of the shadows, she smiled and then hugged and hugged me.

'Thank goodness you're back and in one piece!' she said, which almost made me burst into tears. Then she opened the passenger door.

'In you get, my love,' she told me. 'I'm taking you to your nan's. I rang her after we spoke, even though it was in the early hours. I let her know that I was going to pick you up. She told me straight away to bring you to her. She asked how you sounded and I said all right.'

Well, I might have been up to a point. I still felt stressed after all those terrifying hours and was missing my baby so much. My body was so bruised from Desmond' punches, all I could think about was a soak in a warm bath.

Nan looked so pleased to see me when we arrived at her door. She could hardly thank Carol enough. After hugging me again, Carol said she was going to make her way home. Nan wrapped her arms around me as she brought me in and told me she had already got my bed made. Her tenderness made me cry.

After I had spent nearly a whole day in bed, with Nan bringing me up cups of tea and buttered toast, she advised me to report Desmond's crime of kidnapping and assault at the police station.

'That will give him a lot more trouble,' she said, 'and he deserves it. And before you say no, your reporting him will show social services that you are a responsible parent.'

That wasn't something that I felt able to do well. Knowing social services, I wasn't convinced that they would see it as me being responsible at all. Especially as I had been foolish enough to open that door, but I didn't dare refuse to go.

Nan drove me to the police station that afternoon and told me she would wait outside. I got out of the car and went in, nervously walking over to the front desk. I managed to say there was a crime I wanted to make a statement about. The woman at the desk eyed me up and down, saw that I was pretty young and then placed me in the waiting room. 'I'll get one of our sergeants to see you soon,' was all she said.

I sat and stared at the walls as I waited for the sergeant

to come in. When he did, he took me to another room with a couple of desks in it and sat me down. He had a notebook in front of him and asked me what the crime was I wanted to report.

I can't remember every word I said, but I did call Desmond my boyfriend, which was my first mistake. At least it made his eyebrows rise a little when I told him about being pushed into the car. Then, when I mentioned the B&B and said we were there for the night, his interest in my statement seemed to disappear altogether. The expression on his face when I got to the bit where Desmond had driven me back and let me out of the car so I had to walk in the rain made me realise that I was hardly describing a crime. I just wasn't able to go through the details of what really had happened. Maybe if it had been a female officer sat in front of me, I might have managed a lot better.

I noticed then that he had stopped scribbling. 'I've made some notes on that,' he told me but there was nothing he wanted me to sign. He did finally ask the name of my boyfriend and I noticed that he didn't seem to recognise his name. I can't remember much more apart from being shown out politely.

I stayed at my grandparents' house for a while. Nan, knowing I was missing my baby a lot, was so kind and patient. Three weeks later, I was offered a place at the St Michael's mother and baby assessment unit in Brixton. One part of me could hardly wait to see my son, the other part of me was nervous. I barely knew him by then.

When I moved into the assessment unit, the people in charge there seemed to be doing the same. I felt that every movement I made was being watched and assessed. On arrival, I was told the rules that I had to stick to – I had never heard such strict ones. The biggest one was that, if I wanted my baby to stay with me, I must not have any contact with Desmond or his family. They meant phone calls as well as face to face and, evidently, all the incoming calls were recorded and then listened to. I had to hand over my mobile phone to them as we were not allowed to have one there. To begin with, a member of staff would sleep in my room – I suppose they wanted to see if I fed my son on time. We were only allowed to leave the home for two hours and, if we had gone shopping, we had to show our receipts to prove we knew how to manage money. I managed to follow the rules, for being there with my son made those days with him the happiest ones in my life.

After a few weeks in the unit, I was shown my excellent reports, which stated I was a remarkable mother. I've still kept them so that I can look at them whenever I'm feeling down.

After my time at the unit, I was given a new flat by the council in Watford. 'Just you and me going to live together,' I kept telling my blue-eyed baby boy. Not that he could understand any of my words, but he giggled a bit at the sound of my voice.

When I first left the unit, I stayed with my grandparents for a few days and both of them seemed to love Matthew, and Sid too. Nan went with me to look at the flat and helped me get it ready by ordering some furniture. She also gave me pots and pans as well as some crockery. Her last present was a mobile phone. 'You'll need one,' she told me as she placed it in my hand. 'Your aunts have all chipped in to pay for a good one.'

I felt a little lonely when I moved in. I suppose that was natural after all I'd been through and being in the unit for so long, where I was surrounded by other mothers. As much as I made myself try to hate Desmond, deep down I still yearned for that happy family I had dreamt about since I was a child. I never thought that I would end up as a single mother on benefits, and that made me sad and often very tearful.

Desmond had been arrested yet again just before I went into the unit and he was still in prison. He began sending letters for me to my grandparents' house – I think all of them had 'I love you' on them. I only opened a couple and, after that, I just binned them. I had made myself think that I never wanted to hear his voice or see him again. Everyone who had told me to leave him had been right, I kept telling myself.

One day I went grocery shopping with Matthew in his pram and I bumped into Chanel and Desmond's mum. That was about the last thing I wanted to do.

'Please, Georgia, let me see my nephew,' pleaded Chanel.

'And I want to see my first grandchild too,' his mother said earnestly.

I felt that I could hardly say no to her – after all, he was her first one. I explained that social services had told me that I was not allowed to visit them, nor could they come to where I lived.

They asked for my phone number so that we could arrange to meet up in a coffee shop. 'I'll give it to you if you promise not to give it to Desmond,' I told them. 'Social services have also told me I'm not allowed to phone or take a call from him.'

'Of course we won't,' Chanel assured me.

And as you can imagine, that was yet another one of my big mistakes. At least I had the sense not to give them my address. It only took a few days for them to give my phone number to him. As soon as he got it, Desmond had it placed on his prison pin card and began calling me. Why hadn't I learnt not to trust those two women? They might have missed him when he was inside, but they never seemed to mind that he was such a crook and so violent towards me.

Naturally, his first sentence was a question: 'Now you have my son, when are you going to bring him to see me?'

Perhaps I shouldn't have sounded so angry towards him: 'We're finished. Don't ever call my phone again, and he's not your son, he's mine!'

I changed my number immediately after that.

* * *

In time I started seeing a young guy called Billy. I met him through Niki and felt that it was time to move on with my life. What I didn't know was that Billy had met Chanel several times. He didn't know her that well, but he had chatted to her at a few parties.

Like me, he bumped into her one afternoon and, during their short conversation, my name came out. One of the things I had already learnt about Chanel was that she could be extremely venomous. After Billy had called me his girlfriend, it was enough to make her furious. She was not the type of person who would accept the reasons why I had left Desmond. To her mind I was being unfaithful to her precious brother. She must have decided straight away that she needed to take her revenge. The word 'girlfriend' filled her with anger and hatred towards me.

Chanel made a series of anonymous phone calls to social services, telling them that I was cruel because I left my baby alone and crying while I went out drinking until the early hours. After a few more calls she reported that, when I was drunk, I brought back all sorts of men to my flat. But they were soon wise to her and she was told to stop the calls and that social services were completely aware that none of this was true.

Her next course of action was to keep sending unpleasant messages that filled my inbox. That wasn't enough to crack me, so she made another plan.

Billy came over to my house one night but he had hardly been in more than a few minutes before we heard knocking on the door. He looked through the small peephole then turned and told me it was Chanel with a bunch of tough-looking girls.

'Call the police, Georgia – they're not going to go away,' he said.

So I phoned, saying there was a group trying to break into my flat and mentioning the words 'danger' and 'baby'. That got them saying they would be there in just a few minutes. Social services had always advised that, if a situation like that was to occur, I needed to inform them as well as calling the police.

As soon as I put the phone down, Chanel and her gang began kicking the door and they kept shouting, 'You're a slag!' Luckily for them, there was a window in the hall so they saw the flashing blue light of a police car turn into the small estate where I lived. That made them rush to the front door, still shouting they would get me another time as they left.

The police told me that one more kick to my door and it would have been off its hinges. My brother also turned up, seeing as he was in the force – he must had heard about it on the radio. Sid offered to send someone to fix everything and had a colleague with him who would stay with me until the handymen had finished. He then said that, after all that noise, the baby had picked up my fear and would not stop crying and so, for Matthew's sake as well as mine, Sid would take us to Nan's to stay the night.

'The door will be fixed by the morning,' he promised me.

Before I could report the incident, social services found out about it. With everything else happening, I hadn't remembered that I should have told them. The police had had to report it because of Matthew. So, if Desmond's sister as well as her mother knew where I lived, I must have been mixing with them, it was thought. Despite me explaining that it was Billy – who without realising it – had told Chanel where I lived. I suppose, as far as the social workers were concerned, there was still drama happening in my life, which posed a danger to my child. That was what they must have believed, even if it wasn't true. I never knew what was said by the police.

Social services rang my grandparents' house and made it clear that my son could no longer stay with me. I think if

Grandad had been able to talk to them, it might have made a difference but he was no longer the brilliant man that he had once been.

A meeting was arranged at my grandparents' for the next morning. They began by saying bluntly that they were putting Matthew up for adoption. Of course, Nan tried to argue with them, but she didn't get anywhere.

My Aunt Donna, being a foster carer already, came forward to take my son, which, of course, was better than him being placed with strangers. Nan wanted me to take my story to the papers, insisting there were inadequate grounds for Matthew's removal. She told me they must have wanted to take him away from me from the start. But they needed a reason and Chanel had given them one.

After that meeting, I felt as though my heart had been ripped out and any happiness in my life was gone. Thoughts of losing my baby made me a complete mess. I was still able to see Matthew in Barnet's contact centre regularly, until I was informed that my visits had to be reduced to just once a week. As soon as my son could talk, I heard him call my Aunt Donna 'Mum', which caused me even more pain. My heart was breaking and it took all my strength to stop myself from crying in front of him.

47

After that frightening incident with Chanel and her friends, I called things off with Billy. Once my son had been taken from me, I had little interest in men. I'm sure he must have thought that life with me could mean constant trouble. Although I hadn't been seeing him for long, I was sorry that he was no longer in my life.

I couldn't bear staying in that flat, even after the door was fixed. Although I knew I was physically safe inside, the place had too many memories of my son. For a while I let my sister stay and she completely understood why I didn't want to be there. I preferred to move in with a friend whose home wasn't anywhere near that estate.

When I was only allowed to see my son once a week, my depression only lifted slightly once I was on the train that took me to Southend for that precious weekly visit. I could hardly wait to see my faired-haired boy but now I knew that he would never live with me again. My only remaining hope was that Matthew would stay with Aunt Donna so that I could carry on seeing him.

I can remember only too well the moment in 2007 when his adoption went through. Until then I had hoped that a miracle would happen and that the prospective adopting parents would change their mind. It had been made very clear to me that, once he was adopted, I would never see him again unless, of course, he contacted me once he turned 18.

My life spiralled even more out of control as I tried to wipe out my misery by drinking too much. Most days I would wake with a headache, not even knowing where I was for a while. There were times when I ended up falling sleep on a park bench. When I woke and the day had mysteriously turned dark, I was totally confused, but somehow I managed to get up and stagger back to where I was staying. It was a good thing that my friend was often out and didn't see the state I was in.

It was after Matthew's adoption that Desmond wrote to me. This time it was a long, pleasant and thoughtful letter. He had been released from prison and had already heard that he was not going to see his son again. He finally blamed himself for that. He also told me how drugs had changed him and how in prison he had become clean, which meant that there were no drugs in his body. Once he stopped shaking, as he always did without them, he could see the huge mistakes he had made – 'Bad, selfish ones,' he wrote.

The next part of his letter was a litany of apologies. I had, of course, heard them all before but this time he sounded more sincere – I could almost believe he had gone back to being the man I had first met on that night out with my girlfriends. He also wrote how much he missed me. At the end of the letter was his phone number and his address. 'I would so much like it if we could meet up' was his final sentence.

Somehow I couldn't bin that letter; instead I put it in my shoulder bag and went to the park with a bottle of vodka in my bag. I sat on my favourite bench and sipped away, then pulled out his letter and read all of it again. In the letter he also said how sorry he was that he hadn't had any time with our son. Then I remembered the trouble he had caused in the hospital. He might be blaming the drugs for it, but then, if his son and I mattered so much, he should have stopped taking them. Still, given the amount of drink I was consuming, I thought maybe there are reasons something inside us harms our minds and influences the way we act. By then I had drunk enough to make my legs wobbly and, without thinking, I pulled out my mobile and phoned him. I told him exactly where I was.

His voice sounded both calm and pleased when he said, 'Just give me fifteen minutes and I'll be there, Georgia.'

Seeing as I was pretty drunk when he arrived, I can't remember everything about our reunion. I know I screamed at him about how he had treated me badly and how our lives could have been different. I seem to remember he looked upset about the painful subjects I brought up.

The next thing I knew, he was taking me back to where he was staying. I can't remember much about what we talked about or if we ate anything, but I do know that I foolishly ended up in bed with him. He was good enough to get me back to where I was staying at a reasonable hour, saying that he didn't want my friend to be worried about me.

Another mistake.

Not that I thought about it, I just carried on seeing him. To me, he seemed to be the man I had fallen for at the beginning.

It didn't take long for us to agree to move back into my flat. After another few weeks when no period came, I realised I might be pregnant again. I did my own test, and yes, I was, but I waited a couple of months before I was seen by the same doctor who had tested me before. The hospital gave me the approximate date when I would be due.

When social services found out, they visited my flat fairly quickly. They made it clear that they wanted Desmond and I to be monitored throughout the whole of my pregnancy. If we didn't give them any cause for concern, the three of us could live together.

We knew they would be knocking on our door regularly, which made us decide to move to Southend for a while. The main motive in going there was that the fresh air would be good for a pregnant woman. It was Desmond who found the flat, which was near the sea. 'I've saved some money from my past life,' he told me. 'It's enough to pay the deposit and our rent for some time. I'll look for a decent job as well.'

Our flat was beautiful, the sea was literally at the bottom of our road and the fresh air was as good for me as predicted. I stopped drinking, ate healthily and took myself out walking every day. Lovely as it was, I couldn't stop thinking the whole time that Matthew would have loved it there.

I had been sensible enough to stay within the rules that we

had been given by social services. Which was, if we moved, we had to tell them where we were going until we had proved ourselves to be reliable and good parents. They, in turn, had let social services in Southend know about us and had given them our new address as well as our phone numbers.

We had hardly moved in before they arranged to hold a meeting with us in our flat. They wanted to discuss everything before our baby was born.

I couldn't believe it when they asked if I had obsessive compulsive disorder (OCD) and whether it was affecting my life. Maybe it was because they had seen how tidy the living room was. They even said they thought it was too clean after they had looked in all the other rooms – 'How can a small home be so clean and tidy?' Then one of them noticed that I had a small bruise on my arm, which I assured them wasn't caused by Desmond. I truly didn't know how I had done it and so I just said I had knocked myself against a door when we carried in the boxes on the day of the move. I knew the social worker didn't believe me from the expression on her face and, deep down, I knew I couldn't win with them. This particular social worker had a knack of visiting a few minutes after she had phoned – she couldn't have wanted to give us time to be ready for her.

Finally, the most difficult meeting was just three weeks before my second child was due. This time it was two women who came to the door. They told us that, as long as everything went smoothly, we would be bringing the baby home with us. At the end of what appeared to have been a friendly meeting, one of them brought up a difficult subject: 'We know you have had drug problems, Desmond. Of course, you were clean when you finally left prison but then the prison guards made sure of that.'

I could see the tide of redness going up his cheeks as he replied quite tersely, 'I still am.'

'I'm sure you are, Desmond, but we have to be absolutely sure of that,' the woman told him, 'we need to do a hair-strand test on you – we have to monitor you in these cases.'

Desmond knew what that meant and told me later that he hated the difficult questions. If drugs showed up, they would take back the promise of us bringing our baby home.

Just my luck, I went into labour that very evening and Desmond rushed me to hospital.

My second son, Freddie, was born on 9 August 2008 at 6.15 p.m., weighing 8lb 4oz. He was a healthy baby boy, the nurse told me, and this time Desmond was at the birth. He had stayed at my side for nine hours of labour until the baby finally arrived. The gentle way he spoke to me and held my hand when I was pushing hard made me forget all the past drama and heartache. I felt so emotional and was now convinced that we would at last be the normal family I had always wished for.

When the smiling nurse placed my second son into my arms, I could see he was the spitting image of his brother, Matthew. It was as though history was repeating itself, but at least this time Desmond was there.

Sadly, I would soon find out that history was most definitely repeating itself.

48

Social services arrived at the hospital the next day when Desmond had come back to visit me and our son. They told us that they were going to take Freddie into emergency foster care.

'The problem is that you went into labour so soon, we didn't have time to arrange the drugs test, nor could we manage any monitoring. We will be doing both as soon as we can. That is, if you sign this form agreeing for your son to go into foster care for a while.'

Both of us believed what they told us – we also felt that we didn't have any choice in the matter. But we were definitely fooled by them. They must have already decided that, as a couple, we were not the right people to bring up our child. They knew all about Desmond, his drug usage and his criminal record. In a way, I can almost see their point of view now, but I didn't see it then. I just felt so miserable when I walked into the small spare room, which was all done up for the arrival of my second child. My eyes were almost glued on the empty pure-white Moses basket. I turned from it and opened the little cupboard where the brand-new baby clothes were. That was enough to make my tears flow until I was convulsed with sobs.

While I became completely depressed, instead of trying to console me, Desmond went back to his old ways in no time at all.

'Matthew's gone and so has this new son of mine,' he announced coldly. 'He's not coming back to us. You'd better believe it. They'll get him adopted, as they did Matthew before I even saw him.'

The glare that came my way scared me and I could tell that he was full of blame for me.

A week went by and there was no sight or update from social services.

'They won't come again, their work is done now,' Desmond said. 'Well, at least I don't have to go for that drug test.'

I suppose underneath he must have been as miserable as me. Even so, he had no reason to make me feel even worse. There were days when I was tempted to walk into the sea until the water was over my head. *Don't do it*, my inner voice said and I told myself how upset Nan would be. In reality, I think that was the one thought that stopped me.

Desmond also couldn't handle his grief at losing his son. Whereas I often had tears running down my face, he was just angry all the time. He made one call to social services, only to be told that we had willingly given permission for our baby to be in foster care – which made him clench his fists and swear down the phone.

He began to disappear again, sometimes during the day

and often in the evenings. It only took a few more weeks for me to see from his eyes that he was back on drugs. This time it was a mixture of crack and heroin. When I found out, I wanted to get out and get away from him. Already I knew the effect they would have on him – he could go back to being the man who had beaten me with his fists as well as making me his prisoner.

I didn't have any money or even my bank card – he had managed to get hold of it when I was in the hospital and was the sole earner. He didn't want me to have any independence.

I was right about the drugs changing him back into the man I wanted to escape from. I had thought it would take longer, though. It made his temper uncontrollable and he didn't seem to care about the damage he was doing to a woman who had not long given birth. There was one evening when he was getting ready to go out. 'So, where are you off to?' I said innocently enough. I hadn't thought he would go berserk with me, but he did. He caught hold of me, thumped me so hard that I could hardly stand upright and then he pulled me into the bedroom and forced me to have sex with him. I've tried to block out the memory of it but the pain remains.

I knew I had to get away from him, even if I had no money.

In the morning, when I looked in the mirror, my face was ashen and I had deep shadows under my eyes. I gently removed my clothes, stood in front of the bathroom mirror and saw there were purple bruises all over my body.

Get dressed and think how you're going to get out of here, I told myself as sternly as I could. *No more tears, just work on a plan.* It was then that I decided I was going to fight to get my son back on my own. If I stuck to doing that without Desmond, I would have a chance.

Let's face it, I told myself, *it was being with him that made social services take my baby away.*

So, who could I turn to for help? Why, social services, of course – after all, they had always been nice to me.

I phoned them as soon as Desmond left, slamming the door behind him. I told them I needed help to get away from him and the woman on the phone passed me over to the one that knew me. She didn't even ask what he'd done – I guess she had a good idea what had happened. Her only question was whether he was coming back soon. My answer was that I never knew how long he would be out.

'Right, this is what we must do! We'll bring someone with us who will stand outside and watch out for him. Pack what you can and we'll be over shortly,' she told me.

I threw as much as I could into my case, even though moving at all gave me enormous pain. It was so unfair – this was my home and he was driving me out. When I heard the knock on the door, I flew to it. For once I was pleased to see the two women from social services. They told me if I looked out the window, I would see a large muscular man outside, wearing a green fleece. I glanced out and just seeing him there made me feel so much safer.

The pair of them gave me a hand with the rest of my packing. They had even brought a couple of big plastic bags, which I could fill up so that I didn't have to leave any of my things behind – I even put all the baby's clothes in one of them as I couldn't bear to go without them. In less than half an hour, we were ready to go. After the man walked us up to the women's car, he waited until they drove away.

The refuge looked like an ordinary large house, though I immediately took note of the high wall and gates, which could only be opened from the house.

A doctor had been called to check me over. 'You're lucky you don't have broken ribs, but they're very bruised and you might find taking a deep breath or sleeping very painful,' he said.

I'm sure he gave a lot more details to the warden. He had given me a prescription for tablets to ease my pain and someone from the refuge was immediately sent to the chemist to get them for me.

Some of the women at the refuge had small children, others were on their own, but all of them were welcoming and friendly to me. Talking to them, I began to realise that I was not the only one whose body had been damaged by large fists and feet.

It was after I had been there for a couple of weeks that I had the awful suspicion that I might be pregnant again. I did another test and it confirmed my worst fears. When I had to explain my situation to the woman in charge of the refuge, I was advised to have a termination: 'Your pregnancy is very early, so having an abortion would not present any risk. I'm not going to force you, though. You have a think about it and then you can let me know.'

Back in my room, I sat on the bed and thought about what I should do. My life would be freer, but I just couldn't agree to having that tiny little beginning of a baby removed from me.

I had lost one son completely, but I was still determined to fight for my second son to be returned to me again.

After a while, when my pregnancy began to show, I moved to another women's refuge, this time in London. I was advised that, as Desmond was still in Southend, and even though the police were keeping an eye on him, my unborn child and I would be safer out of the area and where I had family for support.

It was while in the London refuge that I learnt how I might be able to get Freddie back with me. I was told that, if I went to court, I would stand a reasonable chance. Despite being heavily pregnant, I still managed to catch a train to Southend and spent two blissful hours with him in the contact centre. I always took a taxi when I was going there as I didn't want to bump into Desmond and I certainly didn't want him to know about the pregnancy.

I could hardly believe that, even though Desmond was still living in Southend, he hadn't gone to see Freddie once. Yet there was me, travelling across London to the station and getting on the train down there so that I could spend time with that precious child of mine while I was waiting for the court case.

Nan certainly encouraged me to go through with it, even though she was quite annoyed that I was carrying another child of Desmond's. To her, he was nothing but a scumbag. I never did tell her how I got pregnant this time – I knew it would upset her too much. Although the whole of social services knew, I kept quiet about it to my family.

*   *   *

On 8 June 2009, at Chelmsford County Court, I won the case against social services. The fact that Freddie and I would be living with my grandparents evidently helped. I was overjoyed to have him back with me.

49

My third pregnancy was peaceful and flew by in no time at all. No violence, no abuse, just pure love and calm. As I had told Freddie, his baby brother was in there, he would rub my tummy excitedly and try to say 'baby'.

I was so happy and content to be back at my grandparents' home. I had my darling son Freddie and now I could feel my next baby moving inside me. My family were pleased about me being back and they visited often. Finally, I felt then that my life was on the up and up.

Sid told me that Desmond was back in prison again. As usual, it didn't take long for him to start sending me the same type of 'I'm sorry, I love you' letters. Another one came just before I was in hospital having my third boy. I shredded it in front of Nan and then tossed it in the bin.

My son Oscar was born on 9 October 2009 at 3.41 p.m. Like my other two sons, he was absolutely perfect. I sat up the whole of that first night, not letting him out my arms. Even though I had been to court and won my case, I couldn't stop the fear that someone would walk up to my bed and say that he had to be taken into care.

I felt so happy when, walking beside Nan, I went home with my latest little boy. I introduced him to his brother Freddie, who being only 14 months old, immediately put his hand out and chuckled as his fingers touched Oscar's tiny little fists.

I simply loved being with my children. Although I didn't have the happy family unit that I had always longed for, being in the home I had grown up in with them made me feel so safe and secure.

I can't say that the night feeds were easy, they were almost sleepless ones. One child would wake up and then the next one did. Not that it worried me, I just loved every minute of that time and even the dirty nappies and the constant crying didn't bother me. Nor did the huge bags that appeared under my eyes. My little family and I lived at my grandparents' for nearly two years. No stress, no men, no arguments, no substance abuse and no violence – talk about a different life!

If only I could have kept it that way.

50

The council offered me a two-bedroom flat, or rather a maisonette. Nan asked me not to leave and now I wish that I hadn't. But there were two reasons that I felt I should go. First, my grandmother had only just recovered from cancer, which made me feel that two boisterous little boys must be causing an additional strain. I knew Nan loved them, but she needed more rest than they were giving her, although she would never admit that. She was like a mother to me, as well as being my best friend. To this day, I still feel that.

The second reason was that I was beginning to feel I should become more independent and I wanted some time alone when the boys were in bed. During the time I had lived there, Nan had insisted on doing all the cooking, which she was really very good at. I felt that I needed to be more of an adult and should start taking full responsibility for myself and my boys.

Nan, as well as others in the family, offered to have my sons on occasion so that I could socialise. To begin with, I said, 'Thanks, I'll let you know.' I didn't though – I just wanted to spend all my time with my children and maybe it was because I had fought so hard to keep them. Instead, Nan and my friends and family began visiting me at my flat. It was beginning to feel like a proper home.

I decided to open a Facebook account so I could get in touch with some of my old friends online but I couldn't believe it when Desmond suddenly appeared on it. He had used a false name, that of a boy I had known in my class. I had been so careful to only accept people who were genuine friends and now I started to receive hundreds of messages from him and he kept sending me his number.

A number I did not consider ringing.

I blocked him immediately but, of course, it was too late. He begged me on Messenger to let him see his children. I sent a message to him saying that was against everything that I had promised social services. He would have to contact them to get permission, but I doubted he would. They had insisted I sign an agreement that Desmond must not be part of my life while the children were living with me – I was so desperate to have them that I had happily agreed to their conditions.

In the end, Desmond must have got Chanel or a friend to follow me when I went out with the boys – he wanted to find out where we went so that it would look as if he had just bumped into me. He found out that our favourite place was a little park with swings for small children and a cafe which sold ice cream for them and coffee for me.

It was after the boys had been on the swings and I was walking to a bench with a coffee that I saw Desmond rushing over to us. I was so startled, I could hardly move. Of course,

I had no idea of what his real reason for being there might be But he was smarter than I thought. He had brought someone else with him, who remained at a discrete distance. Whoever it was, they must have had a very good camera and, unfortunately, they managed to get some very good – but compromising – photos, including one of Desmond with his arm around my shoulders. I had immediately shrugged it off, but not before that picture was taken. There were others of him bending over the children and all three of them were smiling at each other.

I could hardly tell him to go – I didn't want the boys upset. He stayed around us for about 20 minutes and said how lovely the boys were. Much to my relief, he then walked away.

That was enough for him to have photos to blackmail me.

When I left the park, I hadn't a clue what he was up to. I should have known that there was always some kind of plan in his head for him to control me. I never thought for one moment that he could find out where I lived. Had I forgotten that he had ways of doing just that? I didn't know that, while in prison, he had learnt a lot about computers and how to locate people's addresses.

Desmond waited for a few days before putting his plan into action. He watched me going out shopping and on my return saw how long it took me to unlock the door when I had bags of shopping and a stroller with both my sons in it. Armed with that information, the next time I went shopping, he decided it was time to force his way into our home. I was unlocking the door when he came up behind me. I could hear his breath and, as I turned towards him, I realised it was too late to get away and ask for help.

His hand shot out as before. Only this time it was the door he pushed, so hard that it flew open. 'In we all go,' he murmured as he got hold of the stroller with his left hand. I could see the boys were not in the least bit frightened, they just looked up and smiled – after all, this was the man who had played with them in the park.

His right hand was on my back. 'You go in too,' he said as he gave me a push. Any hope of a neighbour being around who could come to my assistance faded, for one glace told me no one was about.

'Just trying to be helpful, Georgia,' he said.

I knew what that meant – if I didn't step in, I would end up flying through the door, propelled by a very powerful shove.

'Get out, Desmond,' I pleaded. 'You know I'm not allowed to have you here. If anyone sees you, I'll be in real trouble.'

'Oh, Georgia,' he said, 'I've already got something that could cause you a lot more trouble than you can begin to imagine.'

'What are you talking about? I've stuck to all their rules and I've looked after my children well,' I told him.

'You've broken the big one, though, haven't you?' he smirked. 'I've got photos of us meeting in the park. Shows I was playing with my children and you were there, smiling at us. And then there's a really good one of you standing close to me, while my arm's around you.'

Social services were aware that, as badly as Desmond had treated me, I had gone back to him more than once. I knew they would never accept me being with him – even having a coffee out with him and the children would be breaking the law.

He paused to let the enormity of what he was saying sink in before adding, 'If you don't agree with what I want, I'll go to social services with them and complain that it's only them who try to stop me living with you. Both you and my children want me to be here. They would only have to look at my photos to believe everything I tell them. Go on, have a look at them yourself,' tossing them onto the table. 'Don't bother ripping them up, I have another set.'

I felt sick when I looked down at them.

'If you do that and they're taken away, you won't see them again anyway,' I told him.

'Oh, that's not going to happen, is it? You don't want to lose them, but if you throw me out, I'll make sure you do. Now, give me your phone,' he said menacingly.

If I hadn't handed it over, he would have picked up my bag and found it anyway so I did as he asked. He slipped it in his pocket.

My two little boys were still looking up at him, wide-eyed. He bent down, tousled their heads and said something nice to them. Not that I can remember what it was, I was too petrified.

'When you have to make or receive a call, I'll let you do it. But of course, I will listen to what you have to say. And then you will give the phone back to me.'

His presence there and his ice-cold instructions brought on a state of abject fear and confusion. How could I get rid of him without losing my children? Social services knew that I had gone back to him on more than one occasion. I can acknowledge now that he still had the power to control my mind. He was like a drug, and he had been able to do that to me ever since I was 17.

Would I lose my sons if I told social services what was happening when they called to make an appointment? What if I failed to advise them? Would I dare anyway, what with him watching my every move?

51

Desmond had definitely learnt a lot about technology in prison. He installed electronics that picked up all sound within the flat. That meant he could listen to any conversation I had when Nan came over to see me. He also made me believe that, even if he was out of the flat, he could hear us on his phone and that everything was recorded. He could even tell me how many times I flushed the toilet while he was out.

'And if you try to slip a note to her, there's bound to be something you say to tell me what you've done,' he said. 'And you know what I would do then?'

That was a question I dreaded hearing the answer to.

'You hadn't guessed, mmm? I would just tie you up and then take my children with me to somewhere they would never be found. Got it? You better! I made some good contacts in prison and they would help me – you can rely on that, Georgia.'

As he had been through my bag and taken out my biro, I wouldn't have been able to write a note anyway.

The question that I've been asked is why I didn't just walk out when someone arrived? The door wouldn't have been locked then. The answer was I knew he would be back there in seconds. Not being on the ground floor, I just wouldn't have time to get myself and the children out.

I understand now why I was too afraid to ever try that. He had succeeded in making my younger self believe I was trapped forever. Back then, he got me believing all the threats he made would happen if I disobeyed him.

I was pretty thankful that Nan was not able to come over that often. She had enough with looking after her husband, whose dementia had increased, and Grandad couldn't cope with her going out, it distressed him too much. Also, I was scared that Freddie might say something about Desmond to her. Hearing him using the word 'Dad' would hardly please her and it would alert her that he was about.

* * *

There were a few nights when Desmond went out for a short time but, naturally, he locked me in. If only he had left us during the daytime, there might have been people I could call out to for help. I kept looking out of the window when he was gone, but there was no one about in those late evenings.

Apart from him going out for a short time, he never left me alone. He was right by my side when I needed to buy some groceries and when we took the boys back to the park. Being there frightened me as I was scared that more photos of the four of us were being taken.

My small benefits paid for everything when we were out. Desmond was neither claiming his benefits, nor looking for a job. Only later would I understand why. He was on probation, which was the reason he had got out of prison faster than I had expected. Desmond would have known full well that the police would have been informed by the probation service that he had gone missing so, yet again, there was a warrant out for his arrest. He was determined to control me, as well as needing a place to hide in. He didn't think the police would be looking for him in the park and he was crafty enough to make sure we only ever appeared as a couple taking our children out together.

Over the first few weeks he was in my home, he seemed to have changed a little. Even though he gave me no freedom, at least there was no violence or arguments. He played the role of a caring partner and father pretty well and the boys responded well to him. I was just waiting with fear and trepidation for the time when he would turn on me, as I knew he was on drugs. So much for being clean during his prison sentence.

If I had always disliked drugs and the harm they had done to Mum, I hated them even more then. Once he was using more and more, out came his fists and they started landing on me more often. Not only that, he kept telling the boys things about me such as, 'Mummy is a whore.'

What sort of man says that kind of thing to his children?

I slept on the rug downstairs with some cushions. He had taken over my bedroom, which he made me share sometimes, but when I could, I stayed downstairs. He started accusing me of sneaking out and seeing someone else. Whatever drugs he was on, they must have been putting all kinds of unrealistic stories in his head. All I can think is that he must have been losing his mind, which petrified me.

Freddie was beginning to put words together, which worried me. Sentences such as, 'Mummy crying, Daddy, Mummy hurts.' Then that little boy would cuddle up to me and I knew that him hearing his father hitting me was beginning to really upset him.

It's got to stop, I kept saying to myself. I just couldn't think how I could get the help I needed. The worse time I had with Desmond occurred one night after the boys were in bed and I brought out our evening meal. Desmond looked at the food and then began to grumble that he had no cannabis left – he seemed to enjoy smoking it before we ate. I really disliked it, especially as the boys could smell it.

'Give me some cash and I'll make a phone call to get some,' he told me.

I tried to explain that I didn't have anything spare as the amount I got from benefits was only just about covering food and electricity. His response was to swear at me loudly and throw the dinner at the wall. I heard Freddie cry out, which made me rush upstairs to the boys – I didn't want my children to be upset by the noises they had heard. I should have known that his temper would make him much worse.

It only took him a minute to come up the stairs, where he pulled me out of the boys' room and then kicked me over the stair gate. That was the second time he had tried to throw me downstairs, only this time he managed it.

I must have screamed with shock and the pain I felt – I was lucky neither my neck nor my back were broken. What with my screaming and his shouting, it was enough to get both the boys crying loudly. Being a warm evening, the windows were open wide. Our neighbours must have heard all of the sounds of my children crying, me screaming and Desmond shouting. I realised then how our lives were completely messed up. I remembered how upset I had been as a child when there were arguments and violence in front of me – I didn't want my children witnessing the same thing so often that they began to see it as normal behaviour.

I think it was then that I made the decision that, if social services came, I would ask for help. Even if they didn't believe all of what I told them, my children would at least be safe. Doing my best to ignore the waves of pain, I managed to crawl up those stairs again and then, using the rails for support, I got up and, staggering slightly, went into the boys' room. I stayed there until they fell back asleep.

Meanwhile, Desmond was in the living room and ate my plate of dinner. At least he cleaned up the mess.

* * *

The following evening was the last one of us four being together. It began after I had put the boys to bed. When I came back down, Desmond was sitting on the couch.

'You don't sleep with me, but you don't mind spending all your time with my kids, do you? That tells me you love them more than me,' he said.

I did my best not to say anything that would annoy him. 'It's a different kind of love,' I told him, instead of telling the truth, which was that I loved them but by now I hated him. Now, I think even he saw through what I had said and I could tell with just one glance that his temper was rising.

'So, you love me, do you? Well, prove it?'

The next thing that happened was that I was down on the floor with his hands around my neck. I screamed again as my whole body was still hurting from that fall and all I wanted was to lie down peacefully and sleep. At that point everything went blank.

When I came to, my mind was numb. My first thought was, had my boys heard anything? They would be bewildered. They hated seeing me harmed and hearing my cries.

I've got to get out of here, was the only thought drumming through my head.

Later that night, there was a banging on the door. It was locked. I cried out, begging them to wait. They let me know through the door that they were the police and it was Desmond they wanted: 'If he doesn't open the door, we'll have to break it down.'

White-faced and shattered, Desmond came down, carrying a small case. Without looking at me, he unlocked the door. I just felt such a wave of relief that he would be taken away and it would be over.

The door opened and three police officers – two men and a woman – walked in.

Freddie had heard all the banging and the shouts. He was at the top of the stairs crying again and Desmond had not shut the stair gate when he came down.

Desmond passed the case to one of the officers, who glanced

in it. 'I need it with me,' was all he said. As they knew the child could see everything, the police officer spoke quietly: 'For the sake of the children, I don't want to handcuff you. Just come with us now, Desmond, and don't try anything stupid.'

'I won't,' he said and, looking up at his son, he gave a small wave and then left with the two male officers. The woman officer stayed with us.

Freddie came perilously down the stairs, tears streaming down his face. The woman officer went and held his hand and got him down safely. He wriggled into my arms and, once his tears stopped, she told me I should take him back upstairs and put him back into bed.

'I have to take you to the police station,' she told me. 'There are questions they want to ask you.'

'But I can't leave my children alone,' I told her.

'No, of course not. Don't worry, it's under control,' she said.

A few minutes later, there was a knock on the door and two women walked in. I knew straight away that they were from social services.

That evening, to be fair, they did their best to calm me down. They told me it was the neighbours who had rung the police and, because there were children involved, the police rang them.

'As soon as the address came up, we knew who was likely to be living with you. We will have to talk to you later but go with the policewoman now and we'll wait for you here.'

The questions I was asked at the station were mainly about whether I knew Desmond was on parole, but they soon accepted that I didn't. My agreement to not having Desmond in my home was laid down to social services, I was told. They asked why I had broken the agreement, but it was clear to me that they didn't believe my story of how Desmond had forced his way in. I guessed then that he had handed over the photos in that bag that looked as though we were together. They had also worked out how long he had stayed with me. I couldn't make them believe that I had no choice and that he had kept me a prisoner.

Social services agreed with the police. They accepted that I didn't know about Desmond's parole, but they were also of the opinion that I had willingly let him into my home. That meant I had broken the promise I had made. If that wasn't bad enough, the test Desmond was given told them that he was using drugs. They didn't test me because they didn't think that was my addiction, but they told me a little about addicts: 'We all know about drugs and alcohol, but there is one other, which we believe you are. There are women who have been battered and taken into refuges such as the ones you have been to. Do you know the percentage of those women who have gone for help but then go back to the man who nearly put them in hospital?'

I shook my head.

'Over 80 per cent. You don't believe it yet, but that's another form of addiction. And you, Georgia, are addicted to Desmond.'

Over time, I realised that it was true.

As you will have guessed, both those precious children, who I loved so dearly, were taken from me.

52

The day finally arrived for me to have my final goodbyes with my children. My oldest son's face is all I can see every time I close my eyes and I hear Freddie's gentle voice pleading, 'Can we go and live at Nan's house? I love you, Mummy.' My younger boy, Oscar, kissed my head as he babbled away, but he was also in tears at the enormity of the emotion emanating from me.

My heart was breaking. I had fought so hard and Desmond had destroyed everything.

So, did I see him again?

Once.

I cried when we spoke about our boys. Then we walked away, all our losses replaying in our heads. We had ourselves to blame.

I've never seen him since.

* * *

Two years later

My boys were always in my head and, without them, I felt such a deep loss. I did re-establish a relationship with my mum after they left me. Sometimes it was volatile, other times it was close. She still remained an addict, but it was she who encouraged me to have therapy, for I needed help to manage my life going forward.

After some weeks attending therapy, I started a small business. To begin with, I bought second-hand goods. I spent time making them look better and then sold them, making a small profit. I managed to buy a car for £100 and sold it on for £300, having spent hours cleaning and polishing it. After that, my business began to grow. That was the start of me gaining my independence and building my shattered self-esteem.

16 March 2014

This was a sad year and I remember it so clearly. It started when I received the phone call telling me that Mum had had a heart attack. Although I went the hospital as fast as I could, she died before I got there. She was only 47. My brother Sid, more than anyone, touched my heart that day. As you know, he had not been close to Mum because of his attitude to drugs, but I could hear him choking with grief as he talked to her lifeless body. The curtains were around her bed so that those who wanted to say goodbye had privacy, but I couldn't help overhearing. I at least have many memories of her over the years, whereas he was left with very few.

A few months later Grandad died, released from the

dementia that had reduced him so cruelly from the man he was. Although he was far from young, there wasn't a single member of our family who wasn't extremely upset.

7 July 2023

My beautiful aunty and my best friend, Clare, passed away of a heart attack. We were all extremely upset when we heard about it. Nan has always been a brave women, but she must have been completely devastated to have lost her youngest daughter, who was only in her forties.

Today

With the help of my therapist, I have remained strong. At times I've felt so cold, bitter and lonely; I've felt useless and I thought I was a terrible mother. I also wondered how anyone could possibly love me. I have one hope, though, that never leaves me. It is that one day my boys will want to meet me. Each night I go to sleep and dream about them. My heart has been broken, like a puzzle. For now, I need to keep on top of my life, to keep building my career and a future for myself. Ever since Desmond and I met for the last time, we accepted that we would not see each other again. I know I've changed. Thankfully, I'm not the same person any more; I am free from my addiction to him.

I met a new partner and had a daughter, who is nearly four years old now, and she is my best little friend. I live in a two-bedroom, semi-detached house with her. In September 2024, I am starting a degree in Health and Social Science at university, which I hope will lead to a career in social work.

I am also starting voluntary work in a women's refuge. And I still buy and sell cars on the side.

There's not a day that goes by when I don't think about my three lost sons, but for now, I have to be mentally strong and focus on my little girl, who needs me. I feel ashamed that it has taken me until I turned 33 years of age to turn my life around, but I got there in the end. I'm sure there will be many more mountains to climb along the way, but such is life.

I wanted to get my story out, firstly, for my children to hear my side of things, and secondly, to help others who can relate to me in some ways and to let them know that it's never too late to make a change, no matter what your past is, or your age. If you feel you're at rock bottom, my message to you is that I've been there and there's only so far down you can go until you have to come back up.

Acknowledgements

From Toni

Georgia – thank you so much for letting me write your story, and for wanting to do so to help others.

I would like to thank three people who have helped me on my journey: my editor, Ciara Lloyd, my copyeditor, Jane Donovan, and Barbara Levy, who has been my loyal agent for nearly twenty years. Thanks to you all.

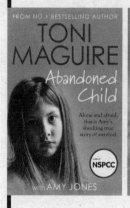

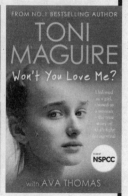